D0969934

a PLACE
and a TIME
A MEMOIR

For Maren
with best wishes.
Bea Mahood
Nov, 2010

BEA MAHOOD

Prologue by BETTY ADCOCK

Copyright © 2010 Bea Mahood
All rights reserved.

ISBN: 1453620532
EAN-13: 9781453620533

For my grandchildren

Grace and Adam Jensen

in memory of my mother

Margaret Marcella Morrow

Contents

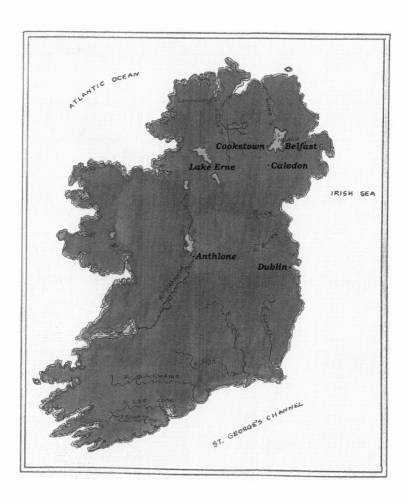

Ireland

Preface

Time slides away, and how are we to taste it?

— May Sarton

I called this book *A Place & A Time,* because it is not meant to be a complete chronicle of our family life at 24 Milburn Street, nor are the events in sequential order. Each chapter was written as a separate essay. These are my memories of growing up in Cookstown, County Tyrone, Northern Ireland in the 1940s and '50s and of the important people in my life.

Our family of eight children was spread out over a period of twenty years. I am the oldest, and left home for Queen's University two years before Trevor, the youngest, was born. I am sure each of my brothers and sisters has a different perspective on this period of our lives. Indeed, it came as a shock to me, when I was writing and reflecting on the past, to realize that Trevor had never known most of the people I was describing.

My brothers and sisters enjoyed reading these essays as they appeared, so with their encouragement and my daughter's, I have finally decided to put them into a small book, along with poems I had written during this time about Ireland and our family, especially my mother. It, therefore, seemed appropriate to include some of the old photographs, retrieved from home and from Granny Morrow's photograph album, and to complete the picture with an abbreviated family tree.

Note: Some people's names have been changed to protect privacy.

Morrow Family Tree

William John Morrow m. Laura Westerman

1904

William Stanley	Harold	Herbert	Lewis John	Joseph
1906-1956				

****

William George Hamilton m. Elizabeth McKinney

George	Joseph	Margaret Marcella (Madge)	Evelynn Elizabeth
		1915-1990	

****

William Stanley Morrow m.
Margaret Marcella Hamilton

1935

Maureen Beatrice	George Harold	Bertha	Noel	Derek John	Clifford Stanley	Irene Marcella	William Trevor
1936	1937	1941	1942	1944	1949	1951	1955

Morrow Great-grandparents

Childhood is a place as well as a time.

— May Sarton

Prologue

A Place & A Time is as the title states, a memoir filled with the detail of a place and an era both divided and part of a whole. Bea Mahood's evocation of life in a rural town in Northern Ireland during the time preceding World War II, extending to her grown-up leaving for parts international and a different life, offers equal parts delight and wisdom as Robert Frost prescribed. The book is both a personal lyric and a loving and sometimes difficult narrative. Beginning with a map of Ireland and May Sarton's beautiful line "Childhood is a place as well as a time," Mahood moves through family history and Irish character with articulate grace.

This reader took a special delight in the author's own very fine poems, a few of which appear at the ends of chapters. Some have seen professional publication. "Necklaces," a brave and beautiful poem, is an especially powerful metaphor of the history of violence and is set around the annual Orange Parade. Then we are also given the sweet wit of "What are ye Ochin' About?" a playful tribute to homemade speech, the soul of place. And the book ends with a poem set in America, in Maine, but "Deer Isle" sings with a particularly Irish depth of sadness and beauty.

Mahood announces at the outset that Northern Ireland, separate from the South and tied to England, is "a young country, but our Troubles are very old." It might be added that the traditions are very old as well. All this is captured in the daily life of the cottage in chapters on "Granny Morrow," "Father and the Animals," "Mondays" and in the accounts of celebration and grief. This book is a gift to the author's family, but it is also a gift to all readers, who may know little of "the other Ireland" and a place and a time that is fascinating, beautiful, sad, and joyous — as childhood is.

Betty Adcock

Family History

We can trace our family history back to our Victorian great-grandparents. A photo exists of the Morrows, sitting in the orchard beside their small, thatched cottage in the townland of Crilly, near the village of Caledon in County Tyrone. Their Christian names and dates have been forgotten, but their time and customs are apparent. It was a Sunday, because all are dressed in their best clothes. Great-grandmother is wearing her black bonnet with its white frill, and holding the open family Bible on her knee. Her husband has his staff of office in his hand, his walking stick made from an ash plant, the badge of a farmer with cattle. Behind them stand their daughters, Martha and Mary Jane.

Their son John married Laura Westerman in 1904. Her parents, Charles and Susanna Westerman, were weavers who moved from Yorkshire, England to Ireland about 1885.

Our maternal great-grandparents, the Hamiltons and McKinneys, came from the Cookstown area. George Hamilton was employed in the linen trade. He married Eliza Speers of Dunman. Their son Willie George, our grandfather on that side, married Elizabeth McKinney. Her parents, Joseph and Margaret, farmed at Toberlane outside Cookstown.

Where I Come From

They change their sky but not their soul who
cross the ocean.

—Horace

A mericans, English and French brim with self-confidence.
I have always envied their self-assurance. The English
have centuries of aristocratic blood to draw on, and the glory
of an empire on which the sun never set still filters through
their language and bearing. The French with their *joie de vivre*
and *je ne sais quoi* pride themselves on their culture, language,
cuisine, Louis XIV and Napoleon. American politicians daily
extol the virtues of this great country and the great American
people while their businessmen stride the world like a Colossus,
flooding it with their latest technology, fast food and American
English.

Those of us who come from small countries lack that
confidence, that sense of national identity. Northern Ireland,
where I'm from, has only been a separate country since 1921
when Ireland was divided in two. It is very small and covers
an area in the Northeast corner of the island, about the size of
Connecticut.

As a country we are very young, but our Troubles are
very old, four hundred years old. But what defines a country?
An artificial border? Size? We don't have our own flag; we
don't have our own passports. Politically we are part of the

United Kingdom, linked to England by a system comparable to that between Puerto Rico and the United States.

Division is our salient feature. Our society is divided in two. From birth we are historically Protestant or Catholic, Unionist or Nationalist. As the wisecrack goes, there is no such thing as an atheist in Northern Ireland. You are either a Protestant atheist or a Catholic atheist.

Part of my lack of confidence stems from the problem of trying to explain where I'm from. If I say I'm Irish, I am assumed to be from the South of Ireland, a country in its own right. I'm certainly not English; British doesn't really fit the bill either. After all, the other countries which make up Great Britain refer to themselves as Scots, Welsh, or English.

So I call myself Northern Irish, but until recently few people had known of the existence of the six counties of Ulster. However, thanks to modern communications we are now as familiar to the TV watcher as Serbia, Croatia, Israel or Palestine. And for similar reasons.

But there you are. It isn't easy being a spokeswoman for a country in such a plight and with such a reputation. For the last thirty years when people have asked me where I am from, I have hated to pronounce the ominous words, *Northern Ireland,* because I am then subjected to a grilling on the Troubles, a euphemism for the sectarian violence that recurs every so often. If I complicate matters further and, because of my blunt nature, admit to being that rare species, a Northern Irish Protestant, I become entangled in a worse web of explanation. I don't look

like a monster, but I am eyed with suspicion. Most Americans
have never before met a Northern Irish Protestant because the
great Irish migrations to Boston, Chicago and New York in the
19th century were mainly Catholic.

Hardly surprising then that in order to avoid the cross-
examination and looks of incomprehension I reply to the casual
question "Where are you from?" with "Cary." The conversation
doesn't rest there, of course, because nobody is supposed to be
from Cary.

"Where did you move from?"

"Belgium," I say, knowing this answer will not satisfy
them either. They are trying to identify the accent that still
lurks around the edges of my voice. It is getting fainter with
the years but is particularly noticeable when I say words like
"rain" or "pain." It's the "ai" sound and the lilt in my voice that
gives me away.

I've arrived in Cary by way of Montreal and Ottawa;
San Juan, Puerto Rico; Paris; Brussels; states as different as
Tennessee and Connecticut, and a six-year stint in the Windy
City, Chicago. Living in these places has blunted my Northern
Irish accent and changed me. I have enjoyed living in countries,
other than my own, where I don't feel compelled to shoulder
the historical burden or defend the actions of my compatriots.
I can appreciate the good and leave or, at least, try to under-
stand the rest.

However, it has also forced me to examine my own
country and realize that what I took for granted is not necessar-

ily the norm anywhere else. The ancient feuds of my tiny country look petty indeed when viewed from thousands of miles away or from another country's perspective. It was a similar shock to my national pride and territorial insularity when I was learning French and Spanish and realized that some expressions in English have no direct translation.

I wondered how these nationalities could live without words for certain ideas and feelings. Even the construction of sentences is different, reaffirming that everyone doesn't think alike. I realized that there are many different ways to express oneself and to live. No one has the ultimate answer except fanatics, but some political systems, some countries, some languages work more successfully or blend more harmoniously than others.

There was a time about the eighth century when Ireland was known as the Land of Saints and Scholars. It has always had a rich tradition of writers and poets. It has always delighted in the spoken word, extolled the gift of the gab. Nothing is enjoyed as much, north or south of the Border, as a good night's *craic*, when people gather round the fire or in a pub, talking, maybe listening to a bit of music or having a dance, but the essential ingredient of the evening is the chat.

Unfortunately, for centuries we have only had the reputation of exporting people or more recently, news of violence and the intransigent speeches of uncompromising politicians entrenched on either side of the cultural divide. However, since the 1960's, concurrent with the renewed outbreak of the

Troubles a plethora of poets has sprung up in Northern Ireland, the most famous of whom is the Nobel laureate, Seamus Heaney.

A literary Renaissance is once again taking place all over Ireland and Irish poets from North and South, Protestant and Catholic, are exposing us to a closer examination of ourselves, giving us new words. Indeed, we may even get to the point where Ciaran Carson's jocular words, *Catestants* and *Protholics,* will no longer be a figment of the poet's imagination.

In October 1998, when Seamus Heaney, with his Northern Irish accent and Ulster expressions read his poetry to a crowd of 1,500 people assembled outdoors on a hot, sticky afternoon at Meredith College in N. Carolina, I realized that finally I could say with pride, "I'm from Northern Ireland."

In the United States Irish poets are teaching in universities from Harvard to Stanford. It's reminiscent of the days of the saints who went forth to establish monasteries across Europe. Is it too much to hope that one day when I say I'm from Northern Ireland, people will look at me with respect and say, "Ah, from The Land of the Poets?"

Bea and the Janus Figure

On Turning Sixty

Our lives are two
If we can relish our past anew.
—Martial

Maybe it was because I was about to turn sixty and could no longer deny my own mortality that my mind turned to the past. It had come upon me as a shock, the realization that my future was shrinking, as if, when I went to the drawer, I discovered my favorite sweater had shrunk in the wash. How could I salvage it?

Grandchildren! They are the link between the old and the young, the past and the present. One of these days perhaps I would have grandchildren. Now that I had thought of this rejuvenating idea, I could hardly wait for my daughter to oblige. But what was I going to hand on to these mythical American grandchildren?

I had always been impressed that Edith Hamilton, the renowned author of books on Greece, had started her writing career at the age of sixty-three. I wouldn't aspire to anything so ambitious, but I would write, I would write for my grandchildren. They would know nothing about Ireland, especially the Ireland where my husband and I had grown up, or its people, their ancestors. And so, the idea of writing memoirs began. Although I had very ambiguous feelings about Northern Ireland and left as soon as I could, I returned many times because of close ties to my mother and younger siblings. I knew I would have many decisions to make when writing about the past. I didn't want to relive the hard times, the difficult times when there wasn't enough money to support a growing family, or the bitterness I felt about my father's drinking habit. I wouldn't write an autobiography or a chronological history of the family but would confine myself to glimpses from the past.

I wanted my grandchildren to know the people who were most important to me, especially my mother and grand-mothers. Although the father's word was law in most house-holds as in ours, these were strong women who held the fabric of their families together. As I wrote and reflected on my early life, I began to appreciate the benefits I'd had. The hard work I so often complained to my mother about had done me no harm, but instead had made me physically strong.

Also I was lucky to have had two grandmothers, each very different in character, who lived within a hundred yards of our house. Their houses were always open to me and reflected their personalities. Granny Hamilton's was a hive of activity, talk and chatter competing with the whirring of her sewing machine.

My paternal grandmother, Granny Morrow, had a strong influence on me, and it was to her I escaped in search of tranquility away from the hustle and bustle of a large family. In the afternoons or evenings I would find her sitting quietly in her armchair by the fire reading a book, knitting or crocheting. When I was young she read to me; then as I got older we played board games or enjoyed a cup of tea together. I listened to her stories about my father and his brothers growing up as I leafed through her photograph album.

Although she had had very little formal education, she read serious literature and could read music and play the harmonium. Her example of independence and love of learning has inspired me as I continue to learn new languages, to write, and to enjoy new intellectual challenges. And I see that same trait woven into the characters and enquiring minds of many of her female descendants.

But it is to my mother I owe the most. It was she who realized that an education was the most important gift she could give to me and my siblings. It was she who worked and sacrificed so that we would have the opportunity for a better life than hers. I find it difficult to write about her and have not been able to do justice to her strong character, her unselfishness, her boundless energy and her colorful turn of phrase. But her words still ring in my ears, and it is to her example I turn when life is tough.

These women would be surprised to find that I have thought them important enough to write about, and to uphold them as examples to a new generation. They would insist that ordinary people have no history, that their lives are not worth writing about, and that it is only in the individual's own family where their influence is felt. And yet I thought if we compare life to a river, we are all like raindrops replenishing its water. Just as the water in the river is constantly changing, so we are all part of the continuum of life.

In the summer of 1997, a year after I had embarked on my writing project, I went to Ireland. While I was there, I visited a small graveyard on the banks of Lower Lough Erne. To reach it I walked down a country lane alongside a field where cows contentedly chewed their cud and stared at me with their large, placid eyes. In the graveyard among weeds and flowers, among stone and marble headstones, stands a squat Janus figure thought to be from the Iron Age.

One face contemplates the gravestones, a reminder of death, the other gazes at the water, a reminder of life. For me it symbolized the enigma of life itself; that in the midst of life there is death. As Montaigne said in his Essays, "Let childhood look ahead, old age backward: was not this the meaning of the double face of Janus?"

Everywhere I went in Ireland I found traces of our Prehistoric ancestors, not only in museums but also in fields, on hills and beside rivers and lakes. And in Sligo an important collection of Megalithic dolmens still stand in a field behind a modern housing estate. Ancient and modern, past and present, side by side. These silent stones, huge and crude, were also burial places, an eloquent testimony of respect for the dead and belief in the mystery of living.

Since writing these memoirs I find that my life has been enriched by looking backwards and forwards, at Ireland's history and my own. Not only have I come to terms with events and relationships in my own past but also with my place in the continuum of life.

Cookstown from the Oldtown Hill

An auction on the Fair Day

Down the Town

Animals, neighbors, treading the pattern
of one time and place into history,
—John Montague

Dr. Cooke's town is often sardonically referred to as "Long Hungry Cookstown" because of its mile-long street that changes names ten times. But just as significant is its topography. Between two hills, Oldtown and Loy, which rise to the north and south lies the heart of the business section, William Street and James Street—everyday names in Northern Ireland except they belonged to the Stewart brothers. After a rebellion in 1641-43 destroyed the original settlement, they rebuilt and extended the town in the early 1700's. Or were the streets named for those English kings, James I and William of Orange, who left such a bitter legacy to Irish history?

Growing up, I lived in Milburn Street on the other side of the Oldtown Hill. My horizons were the hill and Slieve Gallion, the mountain that was such a dramatic backdrop to the town. Like most people in the 1940's and 50's my family didn't own a car; so my world was usually limited to what I could cover on foot. My stamping ground was the Oldtown, but my everyday activities took me "down the town."

Five days a week, four times a day until the age of twelve, I passed the shops, pubs and banks on my way to Burn Road School. At lunchtime I raced home, swallowed my dinner, and tore straight back again in the space of the half hour between 12:30 and 1:00. If I heard the blast of Gunning's Linen Factory horn at five to one and had only reached Eastwood's pub on the corner of William and Orritor Streets, I knew I was in trouble. It was time to pick up my pace and sprint the rest of the way. Just because the potatoes weren't quite ready the minute I flew through the door would not be a good enough excuse for tardiness in Baldy Marshall's eyes.

Walking home after school was a more leisurely process. I sauntered along with my friends and classmates, our numbers thinning out as we went up the main street. Bertie Wilkinson lived above Anderson's, his father's grocery shop; Avril Irwin crossed the wide main street to Coagh Street; and Shirley McGucken said good-bye at the Commercial Hotel. When we reached Milburn Street, Yvonne Gourley continued on down the Moneymore Road. The Blacks, like other farmers' children, continued their long walk to Coolreaghs, and other townlands.

One day I was dawdling home alone, gazing in shop windows, a favorite occupation of mine, even from an early age. Maybe it had been one of Baldy's "Do as you go" afternoons when he assigned sums at the end of the school day. You could go, when you got them right. As I came to Eastwood's shoe shop, a woman approached me. Was I a good pupil, could I read and write well? When I answered in the affirmative, she informed me that she, poor soul, was illiterate and needed a letter written. Would I oblige?

Somewhat unnerved, but being a quiet, shy child, I didn't know what to do but agree. With that she took me by the shoulder and steered me into the nearest entry, where she dictated her letter. I hunkered down and wrote leaning on my schoolbag. She held out the bottle of ink she had so thought-fully brought with her, for we didn't use fountain pens until we were in high school.

The moment I had addressed the envelope, she pressed a half-crown into my hand. By this time, young though I was, I knew she was up to no good and that I had been the inno-cent accomplice to a poison-pen letter. As if the Hound of the Baskervilles was after me, I took to my heels and raced home.

My sorties down the town were not limited to going back and forth to school. As the oldest child in a large family, I was constantly running errands for my mother. I was as familiar with the shops as any adult.

Shops were very different in those days. Before 1948 when most people did not have the opportunity to attend high school, and only a few went to the Tech, working in a shop was considered a good, steady job, if somewhat poorly paid. Like all trades an apprenticeship had to be served, and part-time help was unheard of. Uniforms were the order of the day. In food shops and butcher shops, it was crisp white linen coats; in clothing stores women wore dark dresses or skirts, the men suits.

The town was big enough that even on our side of William Street within a very short distance we had a choice of grocers: Faulkner's, The Home and Colonial, and Anderson's, which Mother, like her mother before her, patronized.

Anderson's was a far cry from the cold, unfriendly supermarkets of today. When you entered the shop, there were no rows of packaged food laid out in self-service cases. Refrigeration had yet to be heard of in either butchers' or grocery stores. You asked for almost everything by weight unless it came in a jar or tin. Mr. McFee, the manager, and Billy Park, his assistant, stood behind the counter in their starched coats ready to serve you. Often the aroma of freshly ground coffee wafted through the shop. Since we only drank tea at home, I didn't realize I was savoring the best part, the smell of coffee being superior to its taste.

Once a week when the order was too heavy to carry home, the shop boy delivered it on his bicycle. Invariably when Jim Park had finished checking Mother's list with her bread-baking supplies, a half stone of flour and an equal quantity of wheaten meal, as well as the usual staples of sugar, syrup, jam, margarine, butter and lard, he asked the same question.

"When would you like the goods sent up? Yesterday, today, tomorrow, the day after tomorrow, Morrow?" I blushed a deep red every time he teased me about my surname, which only added to his satisfaction.

Tea came in wooden chests, the name of the tea and importer stamped in black, stenciled letters. Made of light plywood and reinforced at the corners with metal, empty tea chests had many uses. They were the right size for packing dishes and the like when moving house, and fine enough for doing fretwork.

Flour came by the hundredweight in large, white cotton sacks with the maker's name and that of his product imprinted in red and blue lettering. Flour bags were a much sought-after item by the working class because four bags made a double-bed sheet.

After carefully ripping them apart by unraveling the sturdy cotton thread that held them together, my mother scrubbed, boiled and blued them to remove all trace of writing. Then they were spread out on the hawthorn hedge for the sun to finish the bleaching process. Once restored to their natural whiteness my grandmother assembled them with sturdy run-and-fell seams on her treadle Singer Sewing Machine.

Dried on the line, starched and ironed every week, they were durable, felt fresh and cool, if a trifle coarse. Not until my aunt married did I realize that middle-class people slept on seamless, linen sheets. Nevertheless, in spite of my newly acquired knowledge, when I went to Queen's University, Granny Hamilton's flour-bag sheets accompanied me.

Next door to Anderson's was Alexander's drapery, a shop with which I was very familiar because my grandmother sewed and my mother knitted. It had a long narrow interior with heavy wooden counters on each side of the aisle. The wooden floor resounded and creaked when heavy-footed people walked through the shop.

As you entered, colorful skeins of wool were stacked on the shelves to the right and bolts of material to the left. Women did a lot of knitting in those days, sweaters, socks, mittens, scarves and hats for the family. Dressmakers and tailors still did a brisk business. Ready-made clothes were expensive and beyond the reach of most people.

The men's department was located in the middle section and beyond that were ladies' coats, millinery and underwear. In that more modest day and age privacy was considered necessary for the selection of nightgowns and intimate apparel. Corsets, the best of which were hand-fitted, were worn by all women past a certain age.

In Alexander's and Anderson's, like most shops, employees did not handle money. Overhead was a system of pulleys. Once a purchase was made, the assistant reached up, unscrewed a small wooden cylinder, inserted cash and receipt, replaced it and pulled a lever, which sent it whizzing to the office. Credit was extended to regular customers and noted in a ledger. In shoe and drapery shops goods could be taken home on "appro."

Tuesdays, as well as Saturdays, were busy days in the town. That was the afternoon wives lifted their family allowance at the post office. At Alexander's the pavement was often congested with prams as the women stood chatting or went inside to do their shopping. Prams had to be left outside, but nobody worried about babies being stolen or molested. Indeed, sometimes a mother would emerge with her parcels to find passers-by entertaining an unhappy child.

Located next to Alexander's was Cheever's butcher shop. Kenneth's father in his navy-and-white striped apron and white coat was often to be seen sharpening his knife on a steel, before slicing off a pound of steak for one of the women standing in front of the counter with her basket over her arm.

Like all butchers' shops the tiled floor was covered in sawdust to catch any blood that might drip from the carcasses hanging from black, S-shaped iron hooks against a background of glistening white tiles. In the window limp chickens, their heads drooping, dangled their feet in the air beside strings of pink sausages, above groups of pork chops, dark red kidneys like clusters of grapes, and roasts of beef. It could have been a subject for a still-life painting by one of the old Dutch Masters.

In 1628 Charles I had granted a charter to James Stewart to hold markets and fairs in Cookstown. On Saturdays it lived up to its reputation as a thriving market town, especially once a month when the cattle fair was held. Farmers and their wives drove by in horses and carts, and others came in from the country on bicycles, their shopping bags fastened securely to the back carrier. Creating confusion, droves of cattle mixed with the traffic as they made their way through the town to the Fair Hill.

On that day all around me would be hustle and bustle as I set off to buy mince steak for lunch, or pork fillet for Sunday's dinner at Allen's on Molesworth Street. Hard-working Oldtown housewives were down on their hands and knees scrubbing their front door steps in preparation for Sunday. In front of Armstrong's shop and dairy came the clank of the metal crates and the clink of the milk bottles as men loaded the lorry for the morning delivery.

Over the hill a maid in a pale green overall cleaned the brass nameplate outside McIver's, the dentist's. As I passed McGucken's Hotel, an appetizing whiff of bacon and eggs and the rattle of dishes indicated breakfast was still being served. But the unpleasant odor of last night's stale beer and smoke filled my nostrils when the pub door opened.

It was a welcome antidote to enter the disinfectant atmosphere of McKinney's chemist shop, as it was called before Billy Barnes took over. I handed the empty bottle and a shilling to Jim Henry for a refill of *cascara sagrada* for my grandfather. I would pick it up on my way home.

At Dargan's pub barrels of porter were being rolled up the entry in preparation for the thirsty cattle dealers, farmers and regular customers who would pour in later. I cast a wistful glance at the books displayed in the Mid-Ulster Mail window, but there wasn't much time to indulge in window-shopping. I had been given strict orders to hurry home with the meat for dinner.

One chilly, damp Sunday morning I paused at the top of the Oldtown Hill. The town was deserted except for those, like myself, who were going to church or chapel. I could see all the way to my destination, First Presbyterian Church on Loy Hill. The road snaked, glistening and gray, past the shuttered shops, empty pubs, and tightly locked banks, between the hills of "Long Hungry Cookstown."

What's in a Name?

Christened Beatrice, I was
never mistaken for anyone else in class.
I sat among Violets and Daisies,
frolicked with Avril and May,
entertained Hope and Joy,
envied Helen and Edna
The popular names of the 30's and 40's;
Shirley, Valerie, Yvonne,
they were my closest companions

Margaret and Anne became
Peggy and Nan, but I remained
Beatrice. Too formal for playground
or family banter, it had to be shortened
to B. But how should I spell it—
as an insect or an alphabet letter?
Pronunciation was another matter.
The harsh Ulster consonant accent
swallowed a vowel. My elegant
name became a hissing Bee-triss.
Boys in short flannel trousers
punned on the Beet, then added
a root, and I grew as red as
that unpalatable vegetable.

When I complained of this burden,
Mother retorted,
It's royal, grin and bear it.
I scowled as I scrubbed the linoleum.
Queen Béatrix of the Netherlands
or Queen Victoria's daughter,
what could we possibly have in common?

Retribution at last, for in high school
I was greatly admired.
I played the lead, witty and clever,
in Shakespeare's
Much Ado About Nothing
I could lay claim to literary fame, proudly
bearing the name of Dante's beloved.

Oldtown St. and Milburn St. with Slieve
Gallion in the distance

The Oldtown

Before I built a wall I'd ask to know
What I was walling in or walling out,
—Robert Frost, *Mending Wall*

I grew up in a street whose inhabitants loved walls. They were a status symbol. This was the Oldtown where, on each side of a wide road, rows of two-story, slate-roofed houses climbed the long incline of a hill. At the top middle-class houses were set back from the pavement by large terraced gardens, and at the bottom, where the land flattened out, gardens and houses were smaller but also protected by walls.

Sandwiched in between were the houses of the working-class. Usually these houses had no walls enclosing their minuscule portion of ground. However, four of these, in imitation of their betters, were also fortified with cement walls about three or four feet high. Walls, high enough to keep out any stray dogs, or children who might be playing tag, riding bicycles, scudging hoops or bouncing balls. Walls, low enough for their owners to have an unencumbered view of what was going on in the street. Children, especially boys, loved to use those walls as balance beams, walking or running along their crests with arms outstretched, the daring ones leaping from gatepost to gatepost, but keeping a wary eye out, ready to jump to ground level should an irate owner appear.

In the 1940's and 50's before television drove people indoors, sitting outside watching the world go by was a summer pastime. Each walled house had a garden seat. The rest of us, the non-walled community, sat on our stone windowsills or stood in our doorways, acknowledging the passers-by with a nod of the head, a formal "Good evening," or an ubiquitous comment on Ireland's fickle weather, such as "Lovely evening."

On lovely evenings it was as if the entire population was sitting outside waiting for a performance to start or a parade to come trumpeting over the Oldtown Hill. When it did, we brought out our straight-backed chairs in order to enjoy a grandstand view. But usually there was nothing untoward to feast our eyes upon, just people out for an evening stroll after work. Industrious souls like my mother knitted, but most just gossiped, commented on the passers-by or stared across the street at a mirror image of themselves. To walk up the Oldtown on those evenings past the rows of eyes was like running the gauntlet.

Entries or gateways provided access to the rear of the houses, for all houses, rich and poor, had backyards beyond which stretched long narrow gardens separated from one another by a low hawthorn hedge or a narrow path. Our neighbors to the right, with whom we shared an entry, agreed with Frost's countryman that "Good fences make good neighbors."

Unlike most of the inhabitants of the street the Masons owned their property. Their backyard was enclosed with a stockade of upright railway ties about eight feet tall, and the beginning of their hawthorn hedge was reinforced with chicken wire. There was no danger of snoopers or any need of No Trespassing signs. An equally high stockade separated them from their other neighbor, Mrs. Mason's brother, Tommy Norton, who had right of way across their yard.

Tommy Norton earned his living as a bread man, delivering bread door to door with a horse and cart. Each evening at six o'clock the barricades opened and the horse, released from the shafts, clattered through, his heavy hoofs pounding the hard-packed dirt. But on Saturday nights the huge Clydesdale had to be backed down the entry, through Mason's into his own yard with the bread van behind him. The horse resisted this awkward maneuver, stamping his feet, whinnying, baring his teeth and tossing his head. While Tommy, a small man, cajoled and held him firmly by the reins from the front, Mrs. Norton in apron and house slippers gave quiet instructions on clearance from the rear. After horse and bread van were safely stabled for the weekend, the gates closed as tightly as if it were Buckingham Palace after the Changing of the Guard.

Our neighbors to the left, with whom we shared a backyard with only a path dividing our gardens, were an unmarried brother and sister. Fortunately for us the Hamiltons were extremely tolerant of our large family and animals. They didn't use their garden for anything other than a clothesline so that we had two gardens at our disposal and freedom to play.

To their left occupying the Oldtown's last remaining whitewashed cottage complete with half door and thatched roof lived the Morgans, a family of whom we were terrified. To us they were mysterious figures glimpsed through the screen of a high hawthorn hedge. The mother and grandmother were always clad in black and seemed to us the incarnation of the wicked witches we read about in fairy tales, who lived in thickets surrounded by ferocious animals.

Although some people in the Oldtown still kept hens and chickens in their backyards, and my father even indulged in cows, the Morgans were the last to rear and kill pigs. When the blood-curdling screams of pigs pierced the air, and men's harsh voices shouted orders, I hurried up the garden after my mother with her load of washing. But my younger brothers crouched down behind the hedge, peering through, hoping to witness the gory deed.

Although walls, hedges and fences provided privacy and a certain amount of harmony among neighbors that otherwise might not have existed in such close quarters, "something there is that doesn't love a wall" besides children who have just had their ball confiscated. Divisions in our society existed not only between the classes: rich and poor, gentry and middle class, aristocracy and merchants, but especially between the two different religious and political groups: Protestant and Catholic, or Unionist and Nationalist.

Our end of the town was staunchly Protestant. Other parts were strictly Catholic. In the business section where people still lived above their shops the population was mixed, but in general each group kept to itself and observed the

Lace curtains parted; front doors flew open. Young bloods and hot heads surged into the street, men and women alike. They hurled whatever they could find at the intruders, while others grabbed and punched band members as they scrambled desperately to reboard the moving bus. As it gathered speed, a shower of stones pelted the bus before it disappeared round the Moneymore Road corner. As swiftly as it had started, the excitement was over. But it was a warning of what was to come, for in a few years each side would line up in earnest against the other, and the confrontation would last much longer than a Sunday afternoon.

During the Troubles of the 70's and 80's it was the town itself that needed walls. Instead of a temporary arch erected on the Oldtown Hill for the Twelfth, an inspection post was set up in order to prevent car bombings. Only certain vehicles were permitted to enter the main street. The town for all intents and purposes had returned to the days of a medieval walled city. It was the 90's before peace became a possibility once again.

As times changed, people began to own their houses. The desire for gentrification caused ugly, little concrete walls to spring up like mushrooms the length of the street. Years ago when I was growing up, chestnut trees grew where many of these walls now stand. Rooks proclaimed the arrival of spring from their branches. Boys climbed those trees, while girls skipped in the open spaces, then tied their ropes to the gas lampposts and whirled in and out of the sparse traffic. In autumn we gathered the spiky green chestnut fruit, extracted the nut, seasoned it and challenged our friends to a friendly game of conkers. Later the trees were cut down because they darkened the houses.

Now, gray is the color of the street. Parked cars encroach on the pavement, traffic roars through, and the sound of laughter is forgotten. But rituals and traditions, old animosities have not yet been forgotten. Each Twelfth, white-gaitered pipers still march under the arch in testimony to ancestral victories. And the Lambeg drums reinforce the resolve to "... keep the wall between us as we go."

Assembling for the Twelfth Parade on the
Oldtown Hill, 1915

Necklaces

For Seamus Heaney

The necklace of ancient amber
is old worry beads restrung—
pitted like the mutilated heads
of those Iron Age bodies held
in Europe's peat. The low gleam
of their tannin faces says *blood sacrifice.*
The same righteous cry of the tribe
deadens the scream of the petrified victim
in Gaul or Greece or Macchu Picchu.

In Ulster children gather in crowds
of excitement for the start of the Glorious
Twelfth. Banners, blazing in purple
and gold, crest through the arch.
King William astride his rampant
white stallion swells in the wind
as he crosses the Boyne. Unionist
slogans shout from the border—
Not an Inch, No Surrender.

From the Other Side, a murmur,
its bead roll of tears and martyrs.

A drum major tosses his mace in the air,
kilt and sporran swirling to the skirl
of the pipes and the beat of the snare.
Men in bowler hats, respectably
still sober, parade in Protestant procession
to martial brass and shrill flute bands
and blattering Lambeg drums

Around each neck, an Orange sash.

customs of its tribe and the conventions of society. Parades took place at set times. In Cookstown neither group marched through the other's territory, unlike nowadays when Northern Ireland comes to a standstill as the Orangemen assert their right to march along a Catholic street in Drumcree. The Hibernian Boys stopped short of the Oldtown Hill, and the Orangemen never ventured down Orritor Street.

Catholics celebrated St. Patrick's Day and the Fifteenth of August. The Twelfth of July and the last Saturday in August were the "big days" for us when the Protestant community celebrated its ancient victories over the indigenous Catholic population with Orangemen and Blackmen marching through towns accompanied by bands. An arch decorated with bunting and the Union Jack, the British flag signifying our loyalty to the Crown, was erected across the crest of the Oldtown Hill.

Each July in preparation for the Protestant community's Twelfth celebrations, the Morgan father and son walked up and down their backyard taking turns to blatter a huge Lambeg drum. From the top of the hill the stirring, eerie note of a lone piper echoed their call to arms, but the monotonous sound of the drum dominated and disturbed the peaceful summer evening.

In the 1950's "The Troubles," our euphemism for the sectarian violence between North and South, Protestant and Catholic, reared its ugly head once more. Customs posts were being blown up on the Border between Northern Ireland and The Free State or Eire. Skirmishes were taking place between the IRA and the Royal Ulster Constabulary. The "B Specials," Ulster's Special Forces, were on maneuvers at night.

To us children in the Oldtown it all seemed rather remote and unimportant, just news that grownups listened to on the wireless at six o'clock in the evening, until the sanctity of a dull Protestant Sunday afternoon was ruptured by the sound of a band in the street. We were finishing our dinner after having been to church like most of our neighbors. We looked at one another across the table, eyes like question marks. Who or what could it be? It wasn't the Marching Season.

Father pushed back his chair and thrust the baby at me. My younger brothers scrambled past one another in their hurry to be first out the door. Sounds of yelling and the Nationalist strains of "Forty Shades of Green" entered the house. Father's Protestant Orange blood was up, but Mother issued strict instructions for the door to be shut and for everybody, including Father, to stay inside. She grabbed him by the coat sleeve while I clung to his trouser legs until his loyal, impetuous nature was brought under control.

Soon we learned that a busload of Catholic supporters on their way to a hurley match had dismounted after coming over the Oldtown Hill while their band struck up a rebel tune. Not a soul was in the street because of the hour. Even the neighborhood watchdogs, the Parkers, who sat outside huddled in their coats in the worst weather, had been taken unawares. But "Forty Shades of Green" did not mingle long with the Orange air.

Harold, Bertha and Beatrice, 1942

Clifford, Trevor, Marcella, 1960

From left, Derek, Marcella, Beatrice, Noel
Clifford and Bertha in the striped sweaters, 1952

Derek, Beatrice, Noel, 1957

Bertha, Trevor, Noel, 1957

The eight Morrows, 1990

Father with Harold and Beatrice, 1938

24 Milburn Street

Home is the place where, when you have to go there,
They have to take you in.
—Robert Frost, *The Death of the Hired Man*

I arrived home from the Moneymore Road direction, where the road sweeps gradually downhill around a wide, dangerous corner to join Milburn Street. As the car approached the corner, I was full of apprehension, waiting for the moment of welcome after a long absence.

It was a shock when I saw the house again—the house I had called home for twenty-four years. Everything was so gray—the overcast sky, the road glistening in the weak watery, sunlight and the houses with their wet, shiny, almost black roofs. It had just stopped raining, but I didn't have long to observe the scene before the car came to a screeching halt on the gravel in front of the house.

I knew Mother was waiting for me, keeping busy until I arrived. Impatient to see her, I jumped out of the car, knocked on the door and pushed; it had always stuck because of the damp and was never locked. I entered the narrow hallway which led to the kitchen, noticing the changes. And it had changed.

It was to this little row house that Father and Mother had moved shortly after their marriage in 1935. It was here that the history of our family was written. For the next

nineteen years Father and Mother filled the three bedrooms to
overflowing with children. I was the first to be born in our
parents' bedroom, a pleasant room with two windows overlook-
ing the street, and spent the first few months of my life in the
bottom drawer of Mother's dressing table. The drawer padded
with blankets and placed between two chairs by the side of her
bed, served as a cradle for me and the five brothers and two
sisters that followed me.

Because the house was unheated the bedrooms were
used only for sleeping. On winter mornings when Jack Frost
with his long white fingers had painted his designs on the
windows, we dressed quickly under the bedclothes and rushed
downstairs to the warmth of the kitchen. Usually it was the
only heated room in the house. Only at Christmas a fire lit was
in the parlor, and if someone was ill, a fire was lit in our parents'
bedroom.

When I was young, the kitchen was the focal point of the
house. It was used not only as a living room and dining room,
but also as the place where the meals were cooked, the washing
ironed, and the homework diligently prepared. In retrospect,
I can see that the kitchen was crowded and can understand my
father's complaints about his feet being trampled. How many
people were in that small room at one time—children of all
ages and stages! No wonder he didn't know where to put his
feet without having a child step on his corns.

During the day a pram often usurped the place of an
armchair so that Mother could keep an eye on the baby while

she worked. Mother rarely sat down until after most of the children had gone to bed, and then it was to knit or have her supper. She usually "sat up" very late, long after everyone else had gone to bed, knitting and reading. It was the only time of the day she had peace and quiet, time to "get her head shired."

A large black range dominated one wall of the kitchen and was the source of heat and means of cooking. On Saturdays it was my job to black-lead the range and shine the metal trim with Brasso. Mother baked most of our bread on this coal stove. Irish home-made bread is not made with yeast to make it rise, but with baking soda and buttermilk, and Mother was a very good baker. She made wheaten bannocks in the oven and soda farls on the griddle. Occasionally there was potato bread, which we loved, especially when served with eggs and bacon for tea, or hot off the griddle with the butter melting on it.

Friday was my favorite day because Friday was baking day. Then not only did Mother make bread but also cakes, pies or pastry for Sunday. For some reason I was never asked to make bread, but soon graduated to a responsible role in cake and pastry making. Some of my best memories are of baking with my mother—the smell of the baking bread, the heat of the fire, the cups of tea, and the companionship.

On winter nights the doors to the scullery and the hall were closed to keep out draughts, and everyone huddled round the fire talking, reading, knitting or listening to the radio. Father, when he was in a good mood, sang Irish songs or recited nursery rhymes for us. The youngest child squealed with delight as he dandled it on his foot or knee, chanting "To market, to market to buy a fat pig, Home again, home again, jiggety jig" or "Ride a cock horse to Banbury Cross." He had a good voice and we crowded round his armchair as he sang old favorites like "Cockles and Mussels" or "The Irish Jaunting Car."

On Monday nights, if the weather co-operated for drying the washing, the ironing took place. Because all traffic went through the kitchen, we had to squeeze past the ironing board to go anywhere. Mother liked to chat while ironing, so I often sat at the fire knitting, waiting to take over when she had finished the difficult pieces such as my father's starched shirts with the detachable collars.

Since dryers were unheard of and the Irish weather unreliable when it came to drying clothes outdoors, a system of pulleys was attached to the ceiling opposite the fireplace between the two doors. I hated it when the order was given to "Pull down the pulleys." Then four rows of damp clothes were suspended overhead.

A table with two leaves stood against the wall under the window. There apart from eating, we did our homework. Children were always doing homework or drawing, painting and playing games: Snakes and Ladders, Old Maid and Drafts.

Since my last visit, Mother had renovated the kitchen by knocking down the wall dividing it from the parlor. It was finally a reasonable size. Out had gone the range and in its place was a fire in a grate that one could see; the linoleum polished by hand every week had been replaced by a carpet, and most of the furniture had given way to antiques. An electric stove now graced the scullery, which had been upgraded to kitchen, and the kitchen had now become the living room, although nobody called it that. One by one her children left home, and for nearly twenty years Mother had the "kitchen" to herself.

When I went home for her funeral in 1990, I did not arrive from the Moneymore Road direction as I had always done, but from the opposite end of the town, first seeing Milburn Street from the top of the Oldtown Hill, as we drove past my grandmother's old house. I had been taken directly to the funeral home to see Mother for the last time. A private service was held in the "kitchen." It was full of relatives—and holding onto one another, her five sons and three daughters weeping uncontrollably.

Mondays

Home, and being washday, dined on cold meat.

—Pepys

I hated Mondays! Monday was wash day. The whole house was in turmoil from early morning. Doors and windows were flung open, steam enveloped the kitchen and scullery. Piles of wet clothes were everywhere.

By the time I came down for breakfast, the water was already heating on the black coal-fired range in preparation for the back-breaking work ahead. There was no time to linger over tea and toast, or sneak in a few pages of reading. This was a morning for action. Mother was already rapping out orders.

"Strip the beds."

"Collect the clothes."

"Let's get started before it rains."

Washboards, in those days, were not items for sale in antique shops, nor instruments for musicians in jazz bands. They were part of the essential wash-day equip-ment. First the clothes were scrubbed on the washboard using warm water and soap; before being rinsed. White wash-ing would then undergo a rigorous boiling to remove any lingering stains and to whiten it. Bleach was not part of our arsenal against dirt. No gray clothes hung on our line.

After the clothes were rinsed and wrung out by hand,

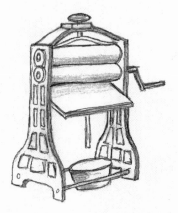

each piece was neatly folded so that it would fit between the rollers of the mangle. Mangling was to the hand-washing process what spinning is to the modern washing machine—a process to remove the excess water.

The mangle, which was housed in the back house, a stone shed in the backyard, was about five feet tall, with an iron frame and two wooden rollers at waist level. On top of the frame was a wheel for adjusting the tension. Mother had set the tension so tight, that the clothes barely fit between the rollers. This made turning the handle a Herculean task.

Once the washing was mangled to my mother's satisfaction (she was a hard taskmaster), and the clothes pegs collected, we proceeded up the garden path carrying the heavy, gray zinc bath loaded with damp, neatly folded clothes.

The garden was long and narrow—at least a quarter of a mile long. Father had left such a narrow pathway between the vegetable patches that there was barely room enough for one person to walk. The wet grass brushed against our shoes as we continued

single file, hanging on to the bath with one hand and trying not to tip the clean washing into the clay and potatoes as we struggled to the top of the hill.

The drying was better there as the wind was stronger. None of our neighbors had their lines at such a distance from their houses and yet, somehow, their washing dried. We did have a great view of the surrounding gardens and fields while hanging out the clothes.

Mother had a system for hanging up the washing in order to conserve space on the line. The corner of one piece overlapped the next one, and the two were fastened with a single clothes peg. To maximize the drying process, each garment was hung by a single thickness of the hem, so that the wind could fill it with air.

The shirts blew back and forth like upside-down scarecrows waving their arms madly in the breeze. Unfortunately, if the wind was blowing too hard from one direction, the washing wrapped itself around the line, frustrating our efforts.

We were at the mercy of the elements. The weather is the most popular topic of conversation in Ireland, and with good reason. Our success in drying the clothes relied on the rain holding off for a few hours. On days when showers were forecast, or the skies threatening and overcast, we had to be alert for the first "spit" of rain.

When the cry went out: "It's raining, get the clothes," we dropped whatever we were doing and sprinted the 440 yards up to the line as if an Olympic gold medal depended on it. Frantically unpinning the washing, we flung the clothes into the bath and charged back down again, while trying to protect the partially dry clothes from the steadily increasing rain. At times it seemed as if we spent half the day running up and down the garden rescuing clothes.

Sometimes a few items left to catch the last of the drying would be forgotten until after dark. Then some unfortunate soul would have to grope his or her way up the narrow path in the pitch dark, legs brushed by wet potatoes and cabbages. If I were the unlucky "volunteer," Father's stories of banshees came unbidden into my head. I tore down the garden, jumping over wet plants, and practically crashed through the back door in my hurry to reach the lighted kitchen and the security of the fireside.

No one ever mentioned being scared to go up to the line at night. However, there were always excuses:

"I have my homework to finish."

"I'm making the supper."

"The clothes are too heavy for me to carry by myself."

I loved school, no Monday washing!

Teatime at Xmas: from left
Mother, Valerie, Marcella and Clifford, 1962

Trevor, Clifford and Derek

Christmas

'Twas the night before Christmas, when all through the house
Not a creature was stirring, not even a mouse.
—Clement Clark Moore

Father loved Christmas, and every year it was he who whipped us into a frenzy of excitement by Christmas Eve. He helped us write letters to Santa and send them up the chimney in a whoosh of air. It was he who got up early with us on Christmas morning and exclaimed over our toys, as excited as any child. When Father said, "It's time to wring the goose's neck," we knew Christmas was not far away.

On Christmas Eve the house was a hive of activity from morning till late at night. Last minute errands were run; Grandfather's tobacco was bought, always the same kind, his favorite blend from Blackley's shop. Half-a-dozen times that day, we dashed up and down the Oldtown to Granny's house and to the shops.

The fruitcake and plum pudding had been made months before and were well matured by now. But the last of the cooking had to be finished, sausage rolls and mince pies baked; cakes iced and trifle made for Christmas tea; cow's tongue, a tradition in Father's family, prepared—served cold on the best china plates, it was delicious. And all day long we pestered Mother and Father with the question, "When can we hang up our stockings?"

The stockings were ready, old stockings belonging to Mother or Grandmother with our names clearly printed on a piece of paper and firmly attached to the top. Mother was still busily working, finishing all preparations for the next day, going back and forth to the range. But we were impatient, and by five o'clock Father had given in. The stockings were hung in a row on the little line just below the mantle piece, and Mother ducked in and out between the dangling stockings as she cooked.

After teatime Father's moment arrived. He summoned the children.

"Time to clean out the goose."

It was a surprise every Christmas. We never knew whether a goose, a turkey, a fat hen or a couple of ducks would grace the festive table. It all depended on what Father brought home. When he worked in butcher's shops, we enjoyed a bird from there. When he was buying and selling cattle, we feasted on a farmyard fowl included in the negotiations over a bullock. Sometimes a goose reared in the backyard adorned the dinner table. To the sentimental among us, it was hard to see the goose we had fed, hanging by its feet outside the back door in the days before Christmas.

But now the butcher was in charge.

"Madge, where's the newspapers? Where's my knife, where's my steel?" Father never looked for anything.

The blade flashed as he sharpened the knife. We gathered expectantly round the kitchen table where the naked goose lay helplessly on a bed of newspaper, staring at us from a glazed eye. We watched in awe as Father, with the skill of a surgeon, deftly, step by step, proceeded to clean out the bird, explaining each step as he went. The goose was now ready for stuffing. Father's work was finished, and he retired to his armchair by the fire.

Now it was Mother's turn. On Christmas Eve, after the bird was taken care of, the stuffing made and the trifle prepared, the fruit cake was iced. The icing of the cake was as important an event as Father's evisceration of the bird and smelt much better.

We always had a decorated fruit cake for Christmas, complete with marzipan and royal icing. It was the "pièce de résistance" of the tea table. Mother's most memorable creation featured a winter scene complete with igloo, Eskimo, fir tree, Santa and the greeting MERRY XMAS in red icing. We thought it the ultimate in cake decorating.

The kitchen and parlor were already festooned with holly, homemade paper garlands, and tissue paper decorations which opened up like little accordions in the shape of bells and balls. Usually we went for walks along the country roads or through the fields with Father to look for holly; he knew the farmers and where the best holly grew.

However, the Christmas decorations changed the year Harold and I were in charge of gathering holly. On our way home after a successful foray to Lissan Plantation, we noticed a small fir tree, a tiny tree, growing in a hedge. We had never had a Christmas tree, and Harold had a brilliant idea. He started hacking the tree with the same implement we had used for cutting the holly branches. It was an old yellow, bone-handled dinner knife sharpened by Mother on the stone windowsill outside the kitchen until the blade was concave. Meanwhile, I, always the worrier, stood quaking in my shoes in case the farmer arrived.

When Mother recovered from the shock of seeing a tree in the midst of the holly boughs, and a scolding, to say the very least, had been administered, the tree was placed on the square bookcase in the corner of the parlor—after all, we couldn't return it. We tied little candles to the ends of the branches and made small decorations out of matchboxes covered with white paper and tied with red wool. And every year from then on, we had a Christmas tree, a legitimate tree.

By nine o'clock on Christmas Eve we had finally been tucked into our beds, and by midnight "Not a creature was stirring." But not for long. Father and Mother had barely settled down for the night before the first anxious pleas began.

"Can we get up yet?"

"Go back to sleep, it's only one o'clock," Father replied, his voice full of sleep. Reluctantly we snuggled down under the blankets once more after furtive whisperings about how to stay awake. And so it went on, all through the night, until Father relented.

Pulling on his pants and rubbing the sleep out of his eyes, he emerged from the bedroom as we tumbled out of bed and raced down the dark stairs in front of him.

"Just a minute, take your time. Let me put on the light."

The squeals of joy and excitement intensified as we rushed toward the fireplace where the stockings hung in a row. What a sight! Toys poked out of Mother's silk stockings, the now-deformed legs strained and stretched at sharp angles all the way down to the great carbuncular toe. Harold, too greedy for a stocking, had hung up a pillowcase, and the baby, unaware of the reason for the excitement, had been allocated one of Father's socks.

Hands grabbed for stockings and presents too big to fit, placed on the sofa and floor. Father was busily taking down stockings for those not tall enough to reach.

"Oh! Look what I got!"

"Are you sure that's yours?" Father admonished the overeager who grabbed presents from the floor. "Whose name was on it?"

And I, the little detective, wondered why Santa's writing resembled Mother's.

Diving into the stockings, we pulled out books, paints, games, chocolates, an apple, and always in the toe a big, fat, juicy orange. Every year we got books: nursery rhyme books, story books, comic books, painting books: games of all sorts, Monopoly, Ludo, Snakes and Ladders, and Happy Families.

There were always jigsaw puzzles which we spent the holidays painstakingly assembling and pondering over where to leave them safely undisturbed. There were dolls for little girls; Meccano sets and trains for little boys.

Father escorted us back upstairs with instructions to play quietly till morning as Mother and the baby were still asleep. How could Mother stay in bed on this, the best morning of the year? Wasn't she excited to see what Santa had brought? I pushed my toys under her nose, but she just opened one eye and muttered something about seeing them in the morning.

We piled into one bed, reading books, playing with toys, admiring one another's presents and eating our chocolates and goodies. Finally getting cold, we separated to our own beds until Mother and Father got up.

After breakfast on Christmas Day, dressed in our Sunday best, we dashed up the Oldtown to deliver presents to Granda, Granny Hamilton and Bella, Grandfather's aunt. Granda was, of course, still relaxing in bed. We stood by the bedroom door and handed over his tobacco. After a few brief words of thanks from him, we swiftly left the frigid bedroom and flew home to enjoy our presents and the warmth of the kitchen and parlor.

We luxuriated in the armchairs beside the parlor fire, toasting our shins and reading our books. Boys sprawled on the floor, playing with tops and trains. We took turns painting at the little table with the curlicue legs in front of the window and were careful not to spill the water.

I looked out between the lace curtains at the gray street with its rows of quiet houses where smoke curled up from the chimneys while Christmas dinners cooked below. A deserted Oldtown met my gaze, very few passers-by, mostly churchgoers. How could people go out on Christmas Day? Why didn't they stay at home and enjoy the luxury of the day? How could children leave their toys, not delve into their books?

To me this was a day to stay at home. It was the only day of the year devoted to children and children's pleasures, a day when chores took a back seat. It was the only time of year when a fire was lit in the parlor, and even more astonishing, we were allowed unrestricted use of it. And it was the only time of year we received presents.

We rarely had snow for Christmas, but the cold, crisp air rushed in through the back door as Father went about his chores of feeding the animals. In the warm kitchen the range glowed as the goose cooked and the plum pudding plumped merrily away amid spirals of steam. And the smells, the smells were delicious. Smells of goose emanated from the oven as it turned golden brown. Rich smells of plum pudding filled the air; exotic smells of cinnamon, cloves, nutmeg and allspice.

As I set the table for dinner, the radio played Christmas carols. I loved Christmas carols but wondered what was so Christmassy about "I saw three ships come sailing by." "Good King Wenceslas" was more my style for secular songs. The rousing "O Come all ye Faithful" and "Hark the Herald" appealed to me and set the tone for the Christmas season, and

I loved the quiet beauty of "Silent Night" and the poignancy of "Away in a Manger."

Father's mother, my favorite grandmother who loved to play games and read books, came for Christmas dinner. At three o'clock the English king delivered his annual Christmas message on the radio to the Commonwealth, while the adults, replete with too much goose and plum pudding, relaxed in armchairs and listened intently.

Mother finally could sit down for a few hours before she started preparations for tea, when her family came. I only remember Granda, who was of a solitary nature, making an appearance once, and Great-great-aunt Bella, dressed in old-fashioned black, always seemed embarrassed to be eating with the men. At teatime we pulled Christmas crackers—a loud bang—and then a little favor, a saying and a tissue paper hat fell out.

Every year as we sat quietly by the fire in the evening, reading and relaxing, tired after the excitement of the day, Bertha would carefully open her box of chocolates and slowly and deliberately place one in her mouth. Every eye was glued to her as she chewed slowly, savoring the taste. We could feel the chocolate melting in her mouth. The rest of us had none of our chocolates, apples or oranges, left; Noel and Derek had devoured their share by breakfast time.

"Give us one, Bertha. Share them with us."

"You each had your own."

"Oh, come on. Don't be so selfish."

"It's not my fault if you..."

Derek, Noel and I exchanged glances, should we tackle her and grab the box? She sensed our intent and clutching her chocolates raced indignantly out of the room calling for Mother as we lunged at her.

And so the day wore on in an atmosphere of warmth, fun, relaxation, good food and the occasional squabble. In the darkness the candles on the Christmas tree were lit. We sat quietly in the firelight marveling at the spectacle and gazing at the flickering lights reflected on the window panes.

Christmas has never been the same since. But every year, in whatever part of the world I happen to be, as I bake the mince pies and boil the plum pudding, I listen to Dylan Thomas reading *A Child's Christmas in Wales*. At the sound of his mellifluous voice and the words "One Christmas was so much like another ... that I can never remember whether ... ," I am transported back to those Christmases long ago in the Oldtown.

Father and the Animals

For each age is a dream that is dying,
Or one that is coming to birth.
—Arthur O' Shaunghessy.

Our lives changed dramatically the day the first cow arrived. No, we had not moved to a farm; we still lived at 24 Milburn Street, in a row house bursting at the seams. Father had inherited some money from his Aunt Mary Jane; instead of being sensible and buying a piece of land, he decided to give up his job in Allen's butcher shop. Now, self-employed with cash in hand, he launched into the cattle-dealing business.

Father was a good judge of cattle, but it was a venture fraught with danger. The buying and selling of cattle was usually conducted at fairs held in different towns once a month. After the deals were made with much spitting and hand slapping, the parties involved repaired to the nearest pub—Father's downfall.

His first purchase was Rosie, a brown cow with white markings. Her job was to supply us and the neighbors with milk and to produce calves. But Rosie required some basic necessities, just as humans do. She needed a house to come home to twice a day at milking time and to stay in during the winter. She needed food: a field to graze in summer, and hay to eat in winter. Our entire vocabulary and chores changed overnight.

Luckily for my father, town planning and zoning were not high priorities for the Cookstown Town Council, for before long major transformations were taking place in the backyard and garden at 24 Milburn Street. Each house in the Oldtown, except for the row of four where my grandmother Hamilton lived, had a hard-packed dirt backyard with a backhouse about twenty yards from the house, behind which a long, narrow garden stretched for a quarter of a mile.

The backhouse, a low, white-washed stone building with a corrugated-iron roof, was used for storage: coal for the range, a mangle for wash-days, garden tools, bicycles and discarded items. No longer! Out went the contents and its conversion into a byre began. First the dirt floor was cemented over, leaving a foot-wide drain just behind the cow stalls. Then a wooden barrier was erected, providing stalls for two cows in each half.

But it wasn't only the back-house that required renovations. In the lower part of the garden new structures were built, albeit of a less sturdy nature than the newly designed, if amateurish byre. Two wooden sheds were constructed: one for cattle, the other for hens. We were going to be almost self-sufficient: potatoes and vegetables from the garden, milk from the cows, and eggs, as well as the occasional Sunday dinner, from the hens.

Once the animals were established on the premises, Father's routine changed. Always an early riser, he was up taking care of the cows before going to fairs all over the North of

Ireland and some in the South—from Lisnaskea to Ballycastle, Auchnacloy to Sligo.

Occasionally he had to leave too early or arrived home too late to milk, and since cows cannot wait indefinitely for the milkman, Harold was taught to milk. Mother refused to learn. She was not an animal lover and, indeed, had more than enough to occupy her indoors. Thankfully, I was never asked. However, there were other jobs in store for me, jobs I came to dread.

Harold, fourteen months my junior, often accompanied Father to fairs during the holidays and on Saturdays. If they had not returned in the evening at the normal milking hour, it fell to me to bring in Rosie. Then Mother and I waited, watching the clock and listening attentively for the sound of their footsteps hurrying round the entry.

Finally, when the cow was bellowing in agony and still no sign of either Harold or Father, action had to be taken. Mother sighed deeply and in tones of resignation said,

"Go, get your grandmother."

Granny Hamilton, now in her seventies, had been raised on a farm. However, she hadn't milked in over forty years, and a few years earlier had been very ill with "pains" (rheumatic fever). She came grudgingly, "chittering" all the way down the Oldtown Hill and while she milked, complaining about the cow and especially about my father.

Instead of being grateful that Granny was doing her best to relieve her misery, Rosie kicked at the bucket and swished her tail in my grandmother's face.

"Madge, hold that cow's tail," Granny ordered.

Backing quickly away in horror, Mother passed the order on to me.

"Beatrice, you do it."

While I stood obediently behind Rosie, gingerly holding on to her tail, Granny crouched painfully on the low milking stool, the bucket between her arthritic knees. Mother stood in the yard, well outside the byre door, offering encouragement as Granny tried to squeeze milk from the unhappy animal. Needless to say, it was not the steady, rhythmic milking of my father, the jets of milk tinging against the sides of the metal bucket and rising in a creamy foam to the top.

But it was not only my grandmother who regretted Harold's occasional absence. When it came to chores concerning the animals, other than milking and going to fairs, I was his reluctant understudy. Sometimes of a summer morning, as I enjoyed my tea and toast and a few precious moments of reading, Mother announced.

"Hurry up and finish your breakfast. You have to take out the cows."

The toast stuck in my throat; my stomach heaved.

"I can't," I protested. "Why? Where's Harold? Where's Daddy?"

"They had to leave early for the fair. You have to do it; there's nobody else. Get a move on."

I was five years older than my sister Bertha, and Noel and Derek were even younger. A mixture of emotions raged through me. I was angry, nervous and terrified. None of my friends had to take out cows. What if I met someone from school? What if the cow ran away? But there was no question of disobeying Mother and if the cows were still in the byre when Father came home, the consequences were unthinkable.

Not a natural with animals, I was scared when I had to squeeze between two of them either to untie or feed them. In winter the cows were kept in the byre and had to be given water and hay, which meant coming dangerously close to their horns. I wasted no time when the cows mooed and turned their heads to look at me with their huge, brown eyes. Father's makeshift byre was not really big enough for four animals, so there was very little space between each two cows and no physical division. The cows were tethered by their necks with one of Father's homemade halters and could move their hind quarters freely.

On one occasion as Harold was feeding them, they locked their buttocks and trapped him. Panic-stricken, Mother dispatched me to find my father's brother Joe, one of the sensible Morrows, who lived a few houses away. Fortunately, he was home and came rushing to the rescue. Shaking his head in dismay after Harold had been safely extricated, he commented, "Stanley'll kill one of the youngsters yet. These fixtures aren't safe."

Since my mother refused to deal with the animals (I think she was scared of them, but no less so than I) I had to untie Rosie before we could proceed for our morning stroll. It was a short distance up Milburn Street to the factory field, a right turn at the factory lane and an immediate left behind the houses.

Rosie knew her way and ambled contentedly along at a sedate pace. She walked on the road while I walked on the footpath, pretending I wasn't with her. Fearful she wouldn't make the turn at the factory lane but head over the Oldtown Hill to freedom and downtown, I dashed ahead to block any false moves on her part. Little did I know that I was increasing the chances of her running away by startling her with my nervous behavior.

But there were worse scenarios. Although Father normally kept only one cow, other "visitors" passed through on their way to and from fairs and customers. Often these heifers and bullocks came from nearby farms or the Cookstown Fair, but the most difficult to handle were those that arrived in a cattle lorry from a fair in some distant town. These poor animals, wild and nervous after traveling for hours huddled together in a confined space, were used to roaming the fields and unaccustomed to traffic.

Our hearts used to sink when word went out that Father was coming up the Oldtown with a herd of cows, or when a cattle lorry stopped in front of the house. As Father rounded up helpers, I kept a low profile. Meanwhile the driver of the lorry and his helper were clambering over the sides of the truck, sticks in hand, separating Father's purchases from the other cattle and guiding them to the back of the lorry.

Amid much shouting and waving of sticks, the hapless animals, nervous and totally confused by now, rushed headlong down the wooden door which served as a ramp. Sentries were posted at all openings to direct them down the entry into the yard, then to the byre or, depending on the number, into the shed at the back. On one occasion, short of help, Father shouted to Mother.

"Madge, come and kep these cows."

With the baby in my arms, I watched quietly from the safety of the kitchen window, hoping I was not the next recruit. As the cattle raced around the yard, Father shouted instructions to Mother, who was standing there terrified. One of the cows, escaping past Mother's ineffectual shooing, turned into our adjoining neighbor's house. Minnie's back door was open. Father cursed and swore, and the rest of us trembled. He yelled at Minnie, whose startled face appeared at the scullery window, to open the front door. Somehow under his guidance the cow exited safely, without damaging Minnie's neat and tidy little house.

When business was in full fling, the factory field was no longer adequate—what with bullocks constantly coming and going and cows having calves. So Father rented the "far" field, located on the "far" side of the linen factory from us. Harold and I had a few scrapes taking unfamiliar cattle to this field. The strange cattle were usually taken out with the docile Rosie who led the way and helped calm the others. Once as we approached the field with our charges, Harold instructed me to go ahead, open the gate and stand guard. Racing past the cows on the bicycle, I accidentally startled one of them. Up the lane, past the gate, into the middle of the traffic on the Orritor Road, it bolted sashaying from side to side.

Cattle can run remarkably fast and by the time the others were safely in the field, the runaway beast was nowhere to be seen. Where could it have gone in such a short time? I was near tears. What if it got hit by a car? We ran up the Orritor Road, asking people if they had seen a stray bullock, but nobody had. We searched diligently in the neighboring fields, telling our story to any farmer we happened to meet, but to no avail. Reluctantly we retraced our footsteps, dreading father's return. It was a "long" day and, yet, too short.

Later Father found the beast grazing contentedly among a herd of cattle in a field previously searched by us. How did he recognize an animal he had just bought the day before? He, who was shortsighted, and never wore glasses? But glasses or no glasses, we were not up to Father's standards. Picking out a suspect from a police lineup would have been easier for me than identifying a steer in a field, especially one I had seen only too briefly from the rear that morning.

But there were other ways of losing cattle, ways unrelated to Harold's and my inexperience and inefficiency. Many a summer's day was ruined for us when news arrived that our cattle had broken out and were wandering the roads or grazing someone else's pasture. If Father was away at a fair, all our activities had to be abandoned as Harold and I rushed off to round up the offending beasts. Then the holes or gaps in the hedges had to be found and plugged up temporarily until

Father arrived. I didn't appreciate my practical experience with the origin of the word "stopgap" and would have much preferred to learn its etymology from a dictionary.

Nevertheless, Father's mood was invariably predictable when he returned home to be greeted by news of the animals' escape, particularly if we had not gone to retrieve them, believing they were safe enough in a farmer's field until he arrived. We were berated for our incompetence. That he did not maintain the hedges properly was never mentioned. A tense silence reigned as he ranted on about the "useless beings he was plagued with ... that he could never count on anybody to do anything ...." At such times I busied myself quietly in the scullery and my breathing did not return to normal until he left, accompanied by Harold.

I thought Father unreasonable in his demands and his complaints about the family never helping him. While it is true that nobody, least of all Mother, shared his zeal for having a farm in the backyard or his enthusiasm for animals of any kind, he was difficult to deal with. A volatile, impulsive man, he rarely planned ahead but expected everyone to be on hand when needed, particularly Harold and then Noel and Derek as they approached the age of usefulness. His quick temper erupted fast and frequently, then simmered down again just as rapidly but left in its wake many unhappy souls.

I thanked the fates I had been born a girl; I had no desire to change places with Harold. At least I was called upon only in emergencies as an unskilled, if reluctant helper. And

much as I hated the drudgery of housework and the confines
of the kitchen and scullery, it was at times like these that
I appreciated Mother's even temperament and the orderliness
of her housekeeping.

Part of the tension between Father and the rest of
the family was due to Mother's and Father's conflicting ideas
about our education. She realized that times had changed and
we should take advantage of the new educational opportunities available to us. We could now become teachers, engineers,
lawyers, architects, bank managers, anything we wanted to be,
if we worked hard at school. Father, on the other hand, still
clung to the tenets and customs of a static, agricultural society.
A son helped his father, as he had done in his father's butcher's
shop. But we lived in the town, and without owning land
being a cattle dealer could never be more than a marginal business. Mother stuck to her guns; we helped Father when we
could, and no-one but he envisaged a return to a rural existence.

Derek, Noel and friend with Miss Ramsey,
our kindergarten teacher.

Donkeys and Other Beasts of Burden

Consider the mule, thick as a stump,
neither one true kind nor the other.
—Betty Adcock, *One of a Kind*

If Father had a fondness for animals, they were anathema to Mother. Indoor or outdoor animals were all the same to her—unnecessary. From the early days of her marriage, she had refused to harbor cats and dogs under her roof. In spite of her admonitions and protestations Father, from time to time, did his best to change her mind and only succeeded in trying her patience.

One Saturday evening when I was very young, Father brought home a gray tabby. The kitchen was spotless, cleaned in preparation for Sunday when no housework was done. The linoleum floor shone around the edge of the coco-mat and the steel trim on the black range gleamed. Late-day sun filtered through the lace curtains, picking up golden lights on the chenille tablecloth, and from the windowsill a vase of fragrant, pastel sweet-peas perfumed the kitchen.

"Stanley, get that cat out of here," Mother commanded. "It's a wild farmyard cat."

"It'll run away," Father protested. "It's scared, that's all."

On Sunday morning we were wakened by Mother's scream. Desperate to escape, the cat had clawed the lace curtains, which now hung in shreds. The flowers lay in damp array on the tablecloth, and the kitchen smelt like a litter box. No church for Father that Sunday. Instead, he was off to the country on his bicycle, the cat in a potato sack, in search of a hospitable farmer.

Not having learnt his lesson and after some time had passed, Father introduced Spot, a fox terrier, to his young household. From its hiding place under the sofa, safe from Mother's wrath, it nipped at our heels. The more we squealed, the more it nipped and yapped.

Relegated to the garden as often as possible out of Mother's way so that she could get on with her work, children and dog kept one another company. But one day while Harold and I were engrossed in our own pursuits, Spot spied a hole in the hedge and dashed into one of the neighbor's yards. There, true to the fox in its name, it wreaked mayhem among McCullough's chickens. Consequently, Father, who was always short of money, had to pay for several dead chickens. And two severely punished children said a tearful goodbye to the terrier.

But once Father had launched into the cattle dealing business, Mother was stuck with animals of the outdoor variety. Instead of spending his days standing behind the counter in a butcher's shop cutting up meat, Father was now out in the fresh air travelling round the countryside, visiting farms and fairs in pursuit of live animals. Rain or shine he was on the road, enjoying himself, negotiating the price of a cow, bullock or heifer.

Opportunities and temptations abounded for him to satisfy his love of animals at every turn, in every field. He could now branch out beyond the conventional small breeds of domesticated animals like cats, dogs and rabbits—for the garden had once been home to a rabbit for a short time. But our enthusiasm for offering it lettuce and cabbage leaves declined when we discovered we were expected to clean out its hutch. We soon realized a rabbit was not the best playmate, and besides, if we let it out, it was in danger of running away.

The goat was a more serious matter. In the summer of 1945 when I was nine and Harold barely eight, Father arrived home from the fair with a white goat. Though technically livestock and saleable, in Mother's estimation it was yet another example of Father's impetuosity and impracticality.

That night, in keeping with his usual, makeshift arrangements, Father tethered the goat to the post of the clothesline at the top of the garden beside Mother's flowers. Next morning, apart from having breakfasted on roses, to our amazement and delight it had produced twin kids. Goat's milk we did not need, for we were already awash in cow's milk, and were turning up our noses at milk puddings for dessert every day—custard, semolina, rice, tapioca and blancmange.

Somehow all of father's bright ideas involved work for Mother, and that summer when the cows' milk was flowing like a river, she had been forced to buy a small, glass hand churn for making butter. But goat's milk! She drew the line at cheese making, and nobody in the family would drink goat's milk because of its strong smell and taste. This animal wasn't going to pay its way even if we delivered cans of its milk to the few neighbors who liked it. However, before it, too, departed, Father found a use for it.

To celebrate VJ Day and the end of World War II, Cookstown, like most towns in Northern Ireland held a parade. All the bands were there—pipe, flute, brass, silver, and tin whistle; military and civil. Anybody that could be was put in uniform. Soldiers and airmen from bases around Cookstown led the parade, followed by women from the WAAFs and WAACs, veterans of the First World War, The Home Guard and The Land Girls. Women of the St. John's Nursing Division stepped smartly out dressed in their navy uniforms and felt hats. Boy Scouts, Girl Guides, Brownies and the Boys Brigade all proudly marched from one end of Cookstown's mile-long main street to the other.

It was better than the Twelfth of July when the Orangemen held their annual parade. This one was nonpartisan, and thanks to the festive, holiday mood the country was enjoying, it included a fancy dress competition. In those politically incorrect days Father decided Harold and our nanny-goat should enter as Gandhi and his goat. At that time the newspapers were full of pictures of Gandhi because of his nonviolent campaign for Indian Independence from the British Empire, and his return to a simple, agricultural lifestyle.

On the big day Harold was accordingly wrapped in a white sheet, his face colored with a paste of water and Bisto, a brown powder Mother normally used for making gravy, and because Gandhi was bald, his hair slicked down with white soap. In a state of great excitement the rest of the family— Bertha who was four, Noel aged two safely ensconced in a stroller, and I—accompanied Mother down the town to watch the festivities.

Not far from the Cenotaph, where the judges and important dignitaries were assembled, we eagerly awaited the arrival of Harold and the goat escorted by Father. To our disappointment they came into view on the opposite side of the street and were oblivious to our frantic waving. However, before long we heard the announcement over the loudspeaker, "Gandhi and his goat, third place." And on Friday their names were published among the list of winners in The Mid-Ulster Mail.

But Father's most memorable and enjoyable purchase from my point of view was made the summer I was twelve. One afternoon he came rushing round the entry, his cap pushed back on his forehead, his face brimming with excitement.

"What do you think I have outside?" he asked. "A donkey."

Mother's face fell. "We don't need a donkey? As if we don't have enough mouths to feed? Another useless animal, good only for eating grass."

But nobody was listening to Mother as we rushed outside after Father to see his latest acquisition. This one was more exciting than most. All the others had involved work of some kind, and boy or girl, we were called upon to participate in the unpleasant chore of cleaning out their living quarters. The donkey would stay in a field, and nature would take care of its sanitary arrangements. Our only acquaintance with donkeys was once a year when we went to the seaside on the Sunday School Excursion. Father always treated us to a ride on the poor animals that spent their days slowly and begrudgingly carrying children up and down the beach.

Except as a source of entertainment for us children, the donkey was an unnecessary addition to a household as impecunious as ours. It served no useful purpose in Mother's opinion, and it had been a long time since anybody in the Oldtown had used donkeys either as a means of transportation or as a beast of burden. Nevertheless, we were the envy of our friends. Even Miss Ramsey, our beloved kindergarten teacher, who lived in one of the fancier houses across the street, had her photograph taken, standing beside the donkey with Noel and Derek, my youngest brothers, on its back.

I don't remember a wet day that summer, though there must have been plenty. All I remember is three of us, my friend Avril, Harold and I, riding that donkey up and down the Factory Field, never tiring of it. I don't remember our giving it a name, but then we probably knew it was not a permanent resident of the Oldtown. Nor was it the most affectionate of animals.

It soon got to know us and lived up to the reputation of its kind for stubbornness and uncooperative behavior. Unlike ponies, that come to the gate in response to sugar cubes and carrots, the donkey was usually to be found skulking at the farthest end of the field among the shadows and weeds. The only time it voluntarily moved with any speed was when it saw us approaching, and raced off in the opposite direction.

But Harold was used to helping Father with cows and bullocks and going to fairs, so he put up with no nonsense from the donkey. Some of his methods were none too gentle. When Avril and I climbed on its back, Harold exhorted it to move by friendly means or foul. A few slaps with a switch across its hind quarters as he pulled and tugged on the rope, usually encouraged it to stumble slowly, if reluctantly, down the field bearing its burden.

The only harness we possessed for the donkey was the bit for its mouth with a short rope attached. Without stirrups it wasn't easy to stay mounted when our steed lowered its head, attempting to throw us. And riding bareback in short skirts was as uncomfortable as sitting on a hacksaw.

Once when the donkey was in a particularly recalcitrant mood, Harold resorted to drastic measures. He twisted its tail, before applying a thorny hawthorn branch to its rear end. The beleaguered animal kicked up its heels and put down its head. As Avril and I went flying forwards, it took off as though it were the favorite in the Grand National.

If horses can be skittish, donkeys are obtuse. Ours refused to walk down the middle of the field unless someone led it. Otherwise, it had its revenge, by clinging as close as possible to the hedge. Hawthorns scratched and nettles stung our bare legs. Once we dismounted, docken leaves were our only cure for the burning itch. As we sat on the grass, rubbing the juicy leaves on our red welts, we chanted "Docken in, nettle out," as Bella had taught us.

(In Latin class that September I learned that the Romans were so desperate for warmth in Britain's cold climate they imported the nettle in order to chafe their limbs. Remembering my smarting legs, I wished they had introduced long trousers instead.)

About three years later Father delivered his coup de grâce. Noel came bursting into the kitchen, where we were doing our homework, breathless with excitement.

"Quick, come on out. You should see Father..."

Homework was abandoned and Mother, who was baking bread, wiped her floury hands on her apron and pushed past us as we rushed to open the front door. For a second even she was speechless.

"Stanley, have you lost all commonsense? Where did you get that contraption?"

There sat Father, proud as a charioteer, at the reins of a pony and trap. If the donkey had been a luxury, this was utter extravagance and even more of an anachronism. In 1950 a few farmers still came to town on Market Day in their horses and carts, but it was rare to see anyone arrive from the country in a pony and trap. In the town anybody who could afford wheels drove a car. This was an antique combination Father would find difficult to resell.

Nonetheless, in spite of Mother's caustic comments and pleas for reason, his enthusiasm remained unabated. The pony was unharnassed from the trap, and the older children took turns riding it up and down the garden under Father's supervision.

The following afternoon, when we arrived home from school, Father was waiting for us, pony and trap in readiness.

"Hurry up. We're going for a ride up the mountain. I have to see a man in Ballybriest about some cattle, and you can all come with me."

The three boys were only too eager to jump aboard, even Bertha climbed in among them, but I hung back in the kitchen. Normally, I would have loved to go to the area around Lough Fea, but in a more modern form of transportation. I was embarrassed to be seen in such an old-fashioned conveyance. There was no refusing Father. Trotting and cantering in our jaunting car along the steep, dirt roads of Slieve Gallion, Father and his charges looked like a scene from the movie, *The Quiet Man*.

It was the first time I had been witness to the rituals of cattle-dealing. The process involved as much haggling and acting as bargaining in an Eastern Bazaar. At one point I was scared, thinking Father and the farmer were about to come to blows, so fierce was the verbal sparring. Finally the price was settled to each one's satisfaction, the hand-shaking took place, and conviviality returned.

After my experience with the donkey I couldn't get used to riding the pony. It was so much bigger and taller, and I felt

I was too high off the ground for safety. Each time it tossed or lowered its head, I was sure I was going to be thrown headfirst and hurt. By now I was fifteen, old enough to understand and sympathize with Mother's frustration and worries caused by Father's charming fecklessness.

For me, the donkey signaled the end of childhood. Avril and I went to separate high schools that autumn, and since we didn't attend the same church, I rarely saw her again. For Harold, the donkey and the pony were just the beginning of a love affair with horses. For Mother, after enduring twenty years of a backyard full of animals, the end was in sight. Her fortitude would soon be tested in a new direction.

The pony was Father's last indulgence. During the next few years until his premature death at the age of fifty, he limited his purchases to the usual procession of cows, calves, heifers and bullocks.

Life with Father, especially for Mother, might often have been stressful, impecunious and precarious, but it was never dull.

Granny Hamilton on her wedding day

Granda and Granny in front of 6 Oldtown Street

Willie George

Like dolmens round my childhood, the old people.
—John Montague

My maternal grandparents lived about one hundred yards up the street from us at 6 Oldtown Street, three houses past the Factory Lane which divided Milburn Street from Oldtown Street. This Protestant section of Cookstown was always referred to as the Oldtown, and my grandfather lived almost his entire life there, moving from one side of the street to the other when he married. He had met my grandmother when he was a tailor and she a tailoress working for the same shop in the town. Granda and Granny Hamilton, as we called them, could not have been more different.

Granny was a talkative, hard-working woman, somewhat scatterbrained, with a fondness for gossip and visiting the neighbors. She spent most of her life sewing, making waistcoats for a tailor's shop and clothes for us and neighbors on an old treadle Singer machine in the kitchen, while squeezing in housework and cooking between callers, gossiping, and most importantly, looking after Willie George, my grandfather.

Treated like a god, he was waited on hand and foot and expected nothing less. Willie George had been raised by his aunts: Bella, Eliza and Maggie Speers and had been completely spoiled by them. Irishmen of his generation were revered.

They were not expected to lend much support to everyday tasks or to the raising of children. That was women's work.

Grandfather was a taciturn, cold, humorless man with whom we children had very little contact—one of the dour Northern Irish, whose ancestors had come from Scotland.

Few of his words were wasted on us, his grandchildren or, indeed, on most of the people who came and went in his house. His only conversations appeared to be with his oldest son George who did his paperwork pertaining to the Ulster Garment Workers' Union.

Of medium height and build, Granda had a middle-aged spread when I knew him. His bald head was crisscrossed with a few strands of white hair and his skin was white and smooth from years spent indoors. It was difficult to associate him with the young man in the wedding portrait in the parlor—the young man with his dark hair parted in the middle, serious face and pencil-thin mustache.

But my most vivid memories of him are after his retirement. Although he spent more time at home than he had when working, he was rarely visible to the rest of the family. During the week he stayed in bed until three o'clock, and on Sundays he never got up at all. All meals were brought upstairs to him in bed. The daily newspaper was delivered to him shortly after breakfast, as soon as my grandmother had time to hurry off to the shop at the top of the hill or send one of us if we happened to drop in.

Not surprisingly, we were often called upon to deliver meals and reading material to him—to save my grandmother's

legs. There we'd find him, propped up in bed, patiently con-
templating the Oldtown, puffing slowly and contentedly on his
pipe while Grandmother scurried around below. The bedroom
reeked of stale tobacco smoke.

When he rose after lunch, everything was in readiness
for his arrival downstairs. His black leather boots stood waiting. Bella, his aunt (who lived with my grandparents after her
sisters died), had cleaned and polished them to a shine that
would have passed inspection by any army sergeant. Water for
shaving was boiling away on the stove. Grandmother and Bella
started fussing the minute he appeared, running to the scullery with the steaming kettle, pouring the hot water into the
washbasin, handing him a towel. (The water had to be carried
in buckets from a pump in the street about twenty yards away.)

The stage was now set for Willie George to begin shaving. First, the razor was sharpened. A thick brown leather
strap about three inches wide hung from a hook on the wall.
Holding the strap at an angle, he stroked, or stropped, the blade
down and up the strap in a long, sweeping rhythmic motion.
My father used safety razors with disposable blades, so we were
always in awe of this performance and watched quietly from the
kitchen. We never dared comment on anything Grandfather
did. Children were to be seen and not heard in his presence.

The straight-edged razor was about six inches long of
the type used in barber shops and disparagingly referred to by
my mother as "your grandfather's cut-throat razor." When he
had carefully lathered his face with the shaving soap and brush,

he peered into the mirror and removed his beard carefully with this dangerous looking instrument. It was not a tool for trembling, shaky hands, but I never remember his cutting himself, and I've often wondered about those mornings when he had over-indulged the night before. He was "fond of a drop," as the Irish say when referring to someone who has a taste for whiskey and Guinness.

As he rinsed the soap off his face into the small basin, it sounded as if an elephant was taking its daily bath at its favorite watering hole. His ablutions completed, he returned upstairs to finish dressing. Men at that time did not have casual attire, and Grandfather descended dressed in his navy blue suit, long-sleeved blue or gray starched shirt with the stiff detachable collar, muttered a few words, adjusted his cloth cap as he passed the mirror in the narrow hall, and headed off down the town for his afternoon stroll and gossip with old cronies. His was a conservative nature whose routine rarely changed, whose movements were unhurried and deliberate.

His walk ended at the shoemaker's. Once there, Grandfather stood in the doorway of the shop, acknowledging the passers-by and stepping aside to let customers enter, or leaned against the counter talking to Tommy Bell, the shoemaker, his half-brother. Tommy Bell sat on a low stool by the window, his leather apron spread across his knees, sewing and hammering away and missing nothing that happened in the main street. The shoemaker's was a meeting spot for old men and nothing of any importance happened in Cookstown that wasn't discussed there.

About ten minutes to six Grandfather returned home  and took his place at the head of the table where his tea was already laid out for him. The radio on the sideboard was turned on in preparation for the six o'clock news which was listened to religiously. As the sonorous chimes of Big Ben filled the kitchen, Grandfather carefully took his gold watch with its long gold chain out of his waistcoat pocket and checked the time. He then glanced up at the clock on the wall to make sure it had not lost a minute.

This clock, which had been a wedding present, was a wall version of the grandfather clock, and was never touched by anyone but him. We were warned against touching the pendulum or jiggling the weights. But they were great temptations for a child as they hung at just the right height, especially if you happened to be sitting in the chair beside them.

Grandfather's last ritual before retiring to bed for the night, was to wind up the "wag-at-the wall" by pulling on the chains, readjusting the weights and resetting the pendulum.

Since Willie George had spent most of his life sitting at a sewing machine or cross-legged on the floor as tailors did in those days, he must have suffered from the sedentary person's problem of constipation. "Moving the bowels" was a very important health concern for many people. It was certainly the only one I ever heard mentioned in connection with him. For this purpose a bottle of cascara *sagrada*, a laxative made from the bark of the cascara tree, was kept on a shelf in the scullery for his weekly dose.

When the bottle was empty, Grandmother dispatched one of us to the chemist's.

"Here's a shilling. Tell Bobby Barnes you want a refill of your grandfather's cascara. And don't drop the bottle."

The bottle had served him well as it had originally been a small hip flask. No one else ever partook of this liquid, always referred to as "your grandfather's cascara." We would have enjoyed the irony had we had known that its proper name was "sacred cascara."

Grandfather took no exercise other than his leisurely stroll down the town, slept in a smoke-filled bedroom and at the age of eighty-nine died peacefully in his sleep without ever having suffered an ache or pain in his entire life. It must have been the cascara that kept him in such good health. That and the fact he had never overworked or wasted energy worrying and had managed to be attended to the end.

There was no need to put R.I.P. on Willie George's tombstone; he had perfected the art of resting in peace many years before.

Bella

The old have a secret,
They cannot tell others, for to understand
you have to be old.
—William Stafford, *Trying to Tell It*

B ella, who came to live with my grandparents after her sister Maggie's death, was my grandfather's aunt, the youngest of his mother's two unmarried sisters. Although Bella did her best to be inconspicuous, Granny Hamilton made no pretense of how she felt about accepting an elderly relative. Bella must have often longed for the privacy and independence of her little house across the street, away from the sound of my grandmother's sharp tongue.

I never knew how old Bella was, but she might have been born around 1870 or possibly earlier, in the middle of Queen Victoria's reign. She had always looked old to me, but then women of her generation looked old long before their time. Most had led hard lives, and so had Bella, who worked in the linen factory like her sisters. Women were required to go into mourning after the death of a close relative, after which they rarely abandoned the black, gray or navy clothes associated with it. And every older woman I knew had her hair pulled back in a bun.

But Bella's dress was more old-fashioned than most. She was a small woman, a little plump and slightly rounded with age. Her rectangular face was deeply wrinkled, her thin white hair was scraped back into a tiny knot, and she was dressed completely in black. Winter or summer her attire never changed. She wore a sleeveless, knitted vest over a long-sleeved, black sateen blouse. A long, black sateen apron hung from her waist to a few inches above the hem of her long serge skirt, which reached to her ankles. Buttoned shoes and thick black stockings completed her outfit. Each Christmas grandmother made her a new blouse and apron. The blouse was a present from Granny and the apron a present from us.

Privacy was an unknown luxury in the Oldtown, because the houses were small and unheated except for the kitchen, where all daytime activity took place. Granny Hamilton sat at the sewing machine. Next to her, tucked into the darkest corner was Bella, occupying the only armchair in the room. There she sat, quietly lost in thought, leaning forward from time to time to warm her hands in front of the fire.

People often dropped by to see my grandmother: sewing customers, relatives and acquaintances from the country, or just plain gossips. Depending on the importance of the caller, Bella was expected to vacate the armchair. If she didn't get up quickly enough, Granny snapped, "Bella, give So-and-so the chair."

Slowly she would rise, resignation apparent in every movement. Rarely did she respond to my grandmother's cutting remarks, but occasionally a pained expression showed in her face or voice. Bella knew her place in my grandmother's house and acted accordingly. Sometimes, as she and I walked arm-in-arm down the Oldtown Hill to our house, I would allude to the incident. But she would excuse my grandmother by saying, "She has a lot to do..."

Although Bella had lived in the Oldtown many years, she never visited any of the other houses. She didn't care for gossip, one of Granny's favorite pastimes. When Charlotte Dunbar, a neighbor and one of my grandmother's cronies arrived, Bella left the kitchen, busying herself in the scullery, or in good weather sitting outside on the windowsill.

She rarely commented on people but would say to me, "That Dunbar!" I don't know why Bella disliked Charlotte Dunbar, but I suspect it was because Charlotte didn't hold Willie George in high-enough esteem. As preparations were made for Granda's arrival by both Granny and Bella, Charlotte, ensconced in Bella's chair and warming herself at the fire would exclaim in disgusted tones, "By Gawd, that Willie George!"

Since my grandmother's house was so close by, I was perpetually dashing in and out on errands, although sometimes I just wanted to escape the never-ending housework and constant caring for my younger brothers and sisters at home. I was Bella's favorite. When I appeared, her face lit up. Often coaxing me to stay by offering me her seat and a cup of tea, she would reach for my hands in cold weather, saying,

"You're freezin'. Here, sit down and warm yourself.."

Then the cream enamel teapot still sitting on the stove was checked,

"Have a sup o'tay, there's some left in the pot."

If the tea was too strong, she added a little hot water from the black kettle simmering away on the stove. But often Mother had given strict instructions for me to hurry home and not dally, and I would have to disappoint her.

At Christmas and on my birthday she took me upstairs to her bedroom and opened the dresser drawer where she kept her pension book and small leather purse. Taking out a shilling or a half-crown, she pressed it into my hand. At other times a coin was slipped into my hand when Granny's back was turned.

"Say nothing to your grandmother," she'd mouth, before Granny would whip round, asking what all the whispering was about. I really appreciated the gifts, for hers were the only birthday presents I ever received, though I do remember Mother once baking me a cake.

Most of Bella's pension was turned over to my grandmother for her keep. Her meager savings were for her funeral. Respectability was very important in the Oldtown and a decent burial was a sign of respectability. "As long as I have enough to bury me," she often said. Before the welfare system, the consequences of poverty were terrifying, either the workhouse or a pauper's grave. Bella had lived long enough to remember those days. The workhouse or poorhouse, as it was commonly called, existed in Cookstown until after the War.

But it was more than the gift of the odd shilling that made Bella special for me. Though she had never married, she loved children. Since I was the oldest daughter, one of my jobs was to look after my siblings. It was rare that I was allowed to go off and play on my own, without brothers and sisters in tow, often including one in a pram.

In those days children were encouraged to play outdoors. In order to finish her work, Mother would chase us outside, or organize us to go for a walk. Walking was a common pastime in Northern Ireland, and we had only to go a few hundred yards in any direction to reach country roads with practically no traffic.

"Can I go and get Bella?" I'd plead.

"Well, don't be long. Hurry up before it starts to rain. Get out while the sun is still shining."

As fast as my legs would carry me, I'd race the hundred yards up the Oldtown Hill, hoping that Bella wasn't in the middle of some housework for my grandmother. I knew she would come if she could.

After all the hands and faces had been washed, the baby fed and ready for a nap, we set off. Bella wheeled the pram, while I held the younger ones by the hand until we turned off the main street. Then we could relax. I would help her push the pram as we chatted. The children, liberated, ran ahead, playing tag, picking up sticks, throwing stones or gathering wildflowers from the hedgerows.

One of our favorite walks was down the Factory Lane, a narrow dirt road between two tall hawthorn hedges, where all we met was an occasional bicycle. In front of the linen factory, a large rectangular pond was home to two beautiful white swans, occasional ducks, and little black waterhens that scurried in and out of the grassy banks. Here we stopped to admire the wildlife and feed the swans the stale bread stowed under the baby's blankets.

In springtime we brought empty jampots to catch tadpoles and sticklebacks. The small shallow pond at the farthest end of the factory was a perfect breeding ground for them. We knelt down and dipped our jars in the water. Many a tadpole perished on the way home, as the water sloshed out of the jars, before they were left to hatch outside on the kitchen windowsill.

Every summer Bella visited the cemetery accompanied by us. It was a long walk especially in warm weather. But once there we rested on the garden seats before visiting the graves. Then a tired tribe straggled home, some complaining about the heat, others constantly inquiring how much farther they had to go and the youngest walker having to be carried.

Spring was skipping time and Bella was in great demand after school, not only as a baby-sitter but also as a rope turner. Patiently and obligingly, Bella sat on the windowsill, keeping an eye on the occupant of the pram and the younger siblings so that I could skip with my cousin Valerie and the neighborhood girls. Two people were needed to turn the rope and Bella could be counted on to turn one end and help keep the chant going.

Tinker, tailor,

Soldier, sailor

Rich man, poor man,
Beggar man, thief.

Probably my earliest memories of Bella go back to
when I was about five or six, when she came to help Mother
by entertaining us on wet days. We played school or shop,
tic-tac-toe and hangman. I was the schoolteacher and Bella did
her sums on a slate and recited her tables like a good pupil. In
her off-key, thin voice she sang songs from long ago about "The
Irish Volunteers" and "Dolly's Braes." On the slippery, brown
rexene sofa Harold, Bertha and I huddled around her, listening
intently to the stories she read us of wicked witches, beautiful
princesses locked in their towers or the little red hen furiously
squawking that the sky was going to fall. We combed Bella's
hair; we climbed all over her. She never lost patience, no matter
how tiresome and cranky we became.

She was also invaluable to my mother when any of the
children were sick. As a baby Derek was seriously ill with double pneumonia before the days of antibiotics. Hour after hour
Bella sat upstairs in my parent's bedroom in front of the fire
rocking him gently back and forth in her arms, softly singing
old lullabies. Afraid he would wake up if transferred to his cot,
she endured cramps in her arms until my mother or I arrived to
relieve her.

In a day and age when children addressed relatives
as Aunt, Uncle, Granny or Granda and all other adults as
Mr., Mrs. or Miss, it is interesting that Bella, whose full name

was Isabella Speers, was always called Bella. But then Bella, unlike other adults, was always kind and caring, never critical. How fitting to realize, after all these years, that Bella means Beautiful.

After a long life and a short illness she died in 1953, the year I went to Queen's University. Years later, on one of my visits back to Ireland, Aunt Evelynn said to Mother,

"Madge, you should give Beatrice the little Victorian ornament Bella left for her. She was so fond of Beatrice."

Bella would be surprised if she knew how many miles her little Victorian boot has traveled and the cherished place it occupies in my house.

Granny Hamilton

Lately I have been thinking much of those,
Through whom life flows
Unstinted, ...
—May Sarton, *Transparencies*

Small, wiry Granny Hamilton could often be seen scurrying down the Oldtown hill, her coat thrown round her shoulders, her head down against the stiff breeze coming off Slieve Gallion, Her familiar bent figure then disappeared into one of the neighbor's houses.

Off on her ceilidh, no doubt, for Granny was fond of a gossip and found many excuses to escape the tedium of hours spent at the sewing machine and the dreary, confined outlook from the kitchen window. The window, hemmed in by sculleries on either side, looked out on the sloping backyard down to the back houses that blocked the view to the field beyond. A half lace curtain filtered what light there was, and beige chintz curtains framed the window.

The kitchen was small and dark with its brown paint, flowered wallpaper and the black iron range that took up half a wall. Its furniture was strictly utilitarian. Only a small armchair tucked into the corner between the sewing machine and range offered any suggestion of comfort. Four straight chairs stood at attention, two at either end of the table and two flanked the sideboard. Grandfather's pride and joy, a wag-at-the-wall clock, loudly ticked away the hours accompanied by the sound of Granny treadling her way through stacks of waistcoats on the Singer Sewing machine.

Not that the beauty of her surroundings or the lack of it bothered Granny, who appeared oblivious to comfort. Granny had been reared on a farm, and the same outdoor, draughty atmosphere pervaded 6 Oldtown Street. Her house, which she shared with her husband Willie George and his aunt Bella, who lived with them for about ten years, was cold and uncomfortable.

While Willie George, unaware of the windswept rooms below, relaxed in bed with pipe and newspaper, Granny flew about the Oldtown. Often, sent up on an errand by my mother, I walked in through the gaping front door to the kitchen, where the sewing had been abandoned in haste. I called her name in case she was in the scullery peeling potatoes for the midday meal, but there was no reply. The backdoor was also wide open. Maybe she had gone to fetch coal for the range, so I hurried down the steep slope to the backhouse and peered into the black gloom, but there was no sign of her. I retraced my steps and climbed the stairs to Grandfather's tobacco-scented bedroom, but he knew nothing of her whereabouts.

Incongruous as it may seem, Granny, who left her house open to the four winds during the day, was meticulous about barring the door at night. It wasn't just a question of locking the door. A sturdy wooden bar, that resembled something you'd find in a barn, slid across the door at night. If we stayed too long, she'd announce it was time to leave so that the door could be barred. We could never figure out what was so valuable in the house other than Willie George and his gold watch. Surely nobody was going to run off with his the wag-at-the-wall clock or sewing machine.

Nevertheless, when Harold slept at her house after Bella died, it became a bone of contention. His bedtime hours were later than Granny's, especially on Saturday nights after going to dances in neighboring towns. When we heard her familiar footsteps coming round the entry or her quick rat-a-tat-tat on the front door, often it was to complain. Harold had forgotten to bar the door; they could have been robbed in their beds.

After her marriage Granny, who had been trained as a tailoress, did piece work at home finishing waistcoats and, from time to time, doing odd bits of sewing for the neighbors. Since all men, rich and poor, wore three-piece suits and most suits were hand tailored, she had a steady, if not lucrative, business.

Granny was not the tidiest of persons and to add to the confusion the kitchen also served as the sewing room. During busy spells it was hard to find a chair to sit on because garments in various stages of completion festooned kitchen and parlor. Panic and pandemonium reigned when a piece of a waistcoat was declared missing. Then the hunt was on, and whoever happened to be there had to join in the search.

"Bella, are you sure you're not sitting on it? Get up a minute."

Poor, long-suffering Bella was unceremoniously dragged out of the armchair where she was quietly minding her own business. While Granny fussed, we, who were always in and out of her house, searched among the myriad pieces of sewing scattered over the kitchen table and sideboard. We checked the parlor where new work was kept and completed waistcoats hung.

Eventually it would be found: under the newspaper, or hidden among the boxes of spools, pins and other accouterments of the sewing trade that adorned the windowsill. Sometimes it had fallen to the linoleum floor, where it was gathering dust among the escaped pins and needles, sewing scraps, and bits and pieces of abandoned thread.

Granny had not been trained as a seamstress. Nevertheless, in addition to tailoring waistcoats and running a house, she was expected to be an expert in sewing everything from dresses to coats, curtains to quilts. The reasoning seemed to be based on the premise that if she could sew a straight seam, she could make anything. And make anything Granny did, including all our clothes, although, sad to say, her labors were not always appreciated by her worst paying customers.

Sometimes commercial patterns were used, Simplicity or Butterick, but more often Granny cut out her own patterns from newspaper or brown paper. But each time she was confronted with a new project, her confidence sagged and she went racing off to consult one of the local dressmakers, such as Mrs. Greer on the other side of the hill. It was the same with knitting socks. She could not turn a heel and had to run to Ginny Bell for help.

When it came to dresses and blouses, collars were her Achilles heel. In every old photograph Granny's handiwork can be detected by the flat collars. Each time she consulted Mrs. Greer, and each collar was invariably—flat. As a child the collars didn't bother me as much as my green coat. I hated the color, a harsh forest green, and how it gaped in front when I walked. Mother complained about the waste of good material, but I had to wear it anyway. Thankfully, it was the last of the handmade coats, so it served two purposes.

Trying on clothes, especially in the early stages when they were held together by pins or a few basting stitches, was torture for us.

"Hold still; put your arms up," Mother commanded as she gingerly eased one of us into the prickly garment.

There we stood half-naked, shivering in the kitchen with strict admonitions not to undo the pins, while Granny, who did not have a gentle touch, tugged and pulled. With her mouth full of pins, she knelt and bent, pinning us into shape, talking and scolding all the time.

"The pins are sticking into me," Bertha or I would wail.

"Stand at peace. Stop fidgeting."

Then she'd call on Mother to turn us into perfect models. Even the boys were subjected to fittings as Granny made all our striped, flannelette, unisex pajamas and their gray-flannel short pants. Meanwhile Mother, oblivious to the cries of her offspring, viewed the garment from all directions and issued her own instructions.

"Let it out ... Take it in ... Shorten ... Lengthen ... The bodice isn't right ... The skirt's too full..."

"Madge, you're far too particular. You can't be pleased. It'll do rightly."

Granny chittered on, but Mother stood firm. She was a perfectionist and lived by the motto "If a thing's worth doing, it's worth doing right." Not so Granny, who believed "A man on a galloping horse will never see it." When we dared complain about a dress or skirt, her curt response was "Be glad you're clad."

Having lost the battle with her daughter, Granny gathered up her bits of sewing and scuttled off back to her sewing machine, but not before she had stopped to console herself with a more appreciative audience. Mother watched her go up the Oldtown, then closed the front door in disgust, saying, "There she goes, complaining to old Bell and giving her all the news."

Granny was well into her seventies, when the lid was finally closed on the old treadle Singer Sewing Machine. The clock now ticked loudly to a silent house. Bella had died a few years earlier, and the piles of sewing were gone. The house was tidy and bare. Meanwhile I had taken up sewing, making my own clothes during the holidays from University and later school-teaching. Granny's first words to me when I came home were always, "Are you coming up to sew?"

When we were young, we didn't appreciate the contribution Granny had made to our lives. At a time when money was a scarce commodity, she had made almost all our clothes, even the sheets we slept on and the quilts that covered our beds. And I didn't know then, that my grandfather had once owned his own tailor's shop but had lost it because of his profligate ways. It was Granny who sewed and worked and kept her family going.

Although neither Granny nor Granda Hamilton ever read anything other than the newspaper nor had any interest in education, it was at 6 Oldtown Street and not at Granny Morrow's that we met our educated relatives. Granny's sister, Aunt Mary Ann, had been trained as a teacher and taught in a one-room school in Toberlane. In those days bright students were tutored by the Headmaster of the elementary school to become teachers. Both she and later Uncle George had benefited from that program. Often after her day's work Aunt Mary Ann cycled in from the country, stopping at Granny's for a cup of tea and a chat, before going down the town to do her errands or visit one of her friends.

Uncle George, Mother's oldest brother, had left school before completing his teacher training, and after serving in World War II, worked in an office. Only two of Granny's four children, Uncle Joe and Mother, left school at fourteen. Joe lived and worked at his grandfather McKinney's farm until it was sold, then drove a van for Inglis Bread. Mother worked in Gunning's Linen Factory until her marriage at the age of twenty.

Evelynn, the youngest of the family, earned a scholarship to the Rainey High School in Magherafelt. She was the first member of the family to attend high school and make the transition to the middle class with her education, job and marriage. Because of her example, Mother realized what a difference education made in one's life. From then on educating her children was Mother's goal. Evelynn was not only intelligent but also good looking with a flair for style. Since Mother was not one to do anything by half measures, we were judged by the standard Evelynn had set in education and style, both in clothes and later on in houses and furniture.

So amid the hubbub that usually prevailed at 6 Oldtown Street, we encountered an interesting mix of people. Traditional blue collar attitudes and the conservative ways and ideas of farmers contrasted with the more enlightened minds of the educated and aspiring middle class. Country met town, and the narrow Oldtown outlook was exposed to the more open views of those, who had lived and worked outside the narrow limits of the Oldtown and Cookstown. It was a preview of the changes to come in society after the War.

Evelynn worked in the Civil Service, where she met and married Reginald Balmer. We now had a bona-fide uncle, who had been a Major during the War. An uncle, to whom the Oldtown seemed like Peyton Place with its gossip and scandals, and better still, an uncle made a fuss of us. Reg was a refreshing change from our other undemonstrative relatives, and Bertha and I used every excuse to hang around Granny's when Reg and Evelynn came to visit.

The arrival of Reg always put Granny in a spin. The sewing was stowed away, the cover put on the sewing machine, and nervous consultations took place about what to serve him. The arrival of royalty could not have engendered more frantic preparations. Linen tablecloths were produced and the best dishes and cutlery unearthed from the depths of the cupboard.

The house at 6 Oldtown Street was a lively meeting place on those Saturday nights when the "quality" came to town. Uncle George arrived first, followed by John Hutchinson, Aunt Mary Anne's adopted son, in from the country for a night's crack. Granda Hamilton, unsociable as he was with the female members of his family, was not one to miss a few free drinks, and escorted the male trio to McGucken's pub, where Reg underwent the rites of passage to the Oldtown.

No one could hold a candle to Granda when it came to drinking, and as Mother said, "You'd be a fool to try." Reg was shocked by the amount Granda could consume, but then Granda had served a long apprenticeship in the Cookstown pubs. While Granda knocked back the black and tans in quick succession, (an Irish whiskey followed by a Guiness), his younger relatives drank at a more leisurely pace. But once there Grandfather ignored them and spent the evening communing with his cronies, only signaling to them with his hand for replenishments.

It was an unsteady group that climbed the Oldtown hill on their way home. Reg arrived all smiles to be greeted by his newlywed's displeased face. Uncle George, who enjoyed a drink in those days, was full of chat.

"The wee women are the worst," he commented—a remark guaranteed to irritate his sister—before the younger men retired to the parlor, where the fire was lit in Reg's honor. This was the moment I enjoyed. Uncle George, egged on by John and Reg, told his war stories, tales of swinging on the vines through the steamy tropical forests of Burma. And Reg, not to be outdone, added his stories of looking for Rommel in the North African Desert. The crack was good, but before long I was sent home to be replaced by Mother, who also enjoyed a diversion from our regular repetitive routine.

Evelynn's displeasure at seeing her husband slightly tipsy in the company of the "Oldtown Ones" was understandable. She had escaped the Oldtown and its drunken ways and had no wish to see her husband corrupted by her father and relatives.

It was a male dominated environment and Reg would have been despised had he not gone. It was important to appear to be one of the boys, even if the boys did not behave themselves. Drinking to excess was common, even when the family suffered because of it, and Grandfather had been guilty of that sin. Evelynn eventually prevailed, George got religion and the Saturday night binges came to an end.

In 1961, six months after I had left Ireland, Granny Hamilton fell in the scullery on the hard-tiled floor. She lay there for three hours until Noel, who had come up to chop sticks for her fire, found her. Unfortunately she developed pneumonia and died in hospital a few days later at the age of eighty.

Granda Hamilton lived on for six more years at 6 Oldtown Street, looked after by my mother and her children.

What are ye ochin about?

I'm homesick for the sound of Irish speech,
the guttural reverberations in the throat
of words like *lough*
that slants its rhyme to cough.

There is a preponderance of *ochs* in talk,
not the clipped polite, Oh yes,
instead, a need to clear the throat
in sentences beginning with *Och aye*.
Is it connected to the weather?

I miss the evening chats around the fire.
Och aye, 'Deed aye, I sigh.
My nostalgia is not
for the weather but the *blether*.

Granda and Granny Morrow with their five sons

Granny Morrow

... the significance of a life depends on the frame that surrounds it.

—Michael Levenson

G ranny Morrow was different, different from all the other people we knew. This remarkable woman grew up during the Industrial Revolution in England and had been subjected to one of its worst abuses—child labor. From the age of eight she attended school half the day and worked in the woolen mill the other half. Yet her intelligence, culture and pride were apparent in everything she did.

Born Laura Westerman on the 18th December 1872 at Holm Villas in Marsden, Yorkshire, she was the fifth child in a family of eight, two of whom died young. Her father Charles was a foreman in the woolen mills, and when that industry began to wane in England, he moved with his family to Athlone in Ireland where his wife Susanna died in 1886 at the age of forty-five when Laura was only fourteen years old.

Some years later the family moved once again in search of work, this time to the village of Caledon, County Tyrone, in what is now Northern Ireland. There they worked in the linen mill as Caledon was a center for processing raw flax into linen thread.

But work was never plentiful in Ireland, and over the years all of Laura's brothers and sisters emigrated. One sister crossed the North Channel to Scotland while the others scattered to the far reaches of the British Empire—Canada, Australia and New Zealand—never to return. Their only contact with their family was by letter, and Laura was a faithful correspondent.

In Caledon she met John Morrow who owned a butcher's shop in the village. Their marriage took place in Dungannon Methodist Church on the 28th December 1904, and in February 1906 their first son Stanley, my father, was born when Laura was thirty-three and John about forty-five. Their generation in Ireland did not marry young, but the next six years were busy and productive as she and John quickly became parents to five sons.

A sixth pregnancy ended in a stillbirth. Although the midwife pretended the baby was a boy, Granny suspected it had been a girl but was not upset. After all, she already had five healthy, strapping sons and was over forty years of age.

She was not one to waste time and emotion on false sentiment or regrets, and her common-sense attitude reflected the harsh environment in which she had lived and, indeed, in which we still lived. Life was tough, especially for women, and another mouth to feed was always a worry in the days of big families.

In the early 1900s there were no welfare systems, no free medical treatment or pre-natal care. Babies were born at home with the assistance of a midwife, the water boiling on the kitchen stove and the doctor summoned only in critical cir-cumstances. Darwin's theories of the survival of the fittest, only too applicable to women in childbirth, were aided and abetted by midwives and doctors in the case of newborns deemed unfit for survival.

But there was something in her remarks that bothered me. There was I, her oldest granddaughter, soaking up everything she said. I, who adored her, who went to her house at any opportunity, being told she was just as glad not to have had a daughter, that girls were nothing but trouble and worry. Her remark rankled, and it was, perhaps, the first time I realized she was not perfect.

When she had first met her sisters-in-law, she thought them backward, practically uncivilized in her eyes. Ireland was always fifty years behind the times, especially then, partly because of its remote, insular location and lack of large towns. Her in-laws, small farmers, lived in primitive conditions in rural surroundings in the same manner they had been living for centuries, cultivating small fields and keeping a few cattle and hens.

Laura instructed them in the sophisticated ways of England and the city of Athlone, even introducing them to the wearing of bloomers. In spite of her initial opinion of them, Grandmother continued to visit Great-aunt Mary Jane, the sole survivor of that generation of Morrows, after she came to Cookstown.

But Grandmother never forgot she was English and felt innately superior to the Irish. And I was so parochial in my view of the world that when I realized she was English, I felt betrayed.

Granny often talked to me about the past as we sat by the parlor fire while I pored over the family Bible and her photograph album, asking questions. I was curious about the women in long skirts and puffy sleeves, about the people who had emigrated and sent back photographs of themselves in the snows of Canada or the tropics of Australia. For me they had the romance of a far-off time or place.

No less interesting but more terrifying were her stories of life in Caledon in the early 1900s. Those were dangerous times when the "Troubles" were at their worst, when skirmishes between the IRA and the Unionists protruded into ordinary people's lives. Where in the early mornings, IRA gunmen kidnapped farmers as they went to milk their cows, where during outbursts of sporadic gunfire, shots whistled across the fields as men worked.

I loved to listen to her reminisce about my father and his brothers growing up in the house above the butcher's shop and of their life in this tiny feudal village. I was fascinated by the photographs of Caledon. There was one of the small-gauge Clogher Valley railroad with the train halted in the middle of the snow-covered Main Street, surrounded by people in old-fashioned clothes.

There were pictures of the little stone schoolhouse, of the monument erected by the villagers in honor of the Lord Caledon who had distinguished himself in the First World War and of the castle where the present Lord Caledon lived. Granny informed me he had been an important general known as Field

Marshal Alexander during World War II and that Northern Ireland had produced two other notable generals in that war, Montgomery and Allenbrooke. She instilled in me a sense of pride: in the family, in Caledon, in Northern Ireland, and ultimately in myself.

But her most intriguing story was her explanation of how she had named her sons. William Stanley, the eldest, was endowed with the illustrious names of William the Conqueror and Stanley the explorer in order to ensure outstanding qualities in him.

Harold, her second son, bore the noble name of Harold, Earl of Essex, the last Saxon king of England, defeated at the battle of Hastings in 1066 by William the Conqueror. Herbert, her middle son, had the strange and surprising middle name of Pharoh. Grandfather, when registering his son's birth, impulsively decided to include a Biblical name to please his wife, misspelling it in the process. Indignantly, on his return, she informed him that Pharaoh was not an acceptable name, not even Christian; Pharaoh was pagan, the title of an Egyptian ruler. Immediately, he was dispatched to rectify his mistake; but the authorities refused. Needless to say, while Pharaoh may have been his legal name, Herbert was not christened Pharaoh, just plain Herbert.

No such liberty was granted Grandfather in the case of Lewis, for whom she chose the names of the Sun King, Louis XIV, and John the Baptist. Joseph, the youngest, was given a prestigious model to emulate in Joseph and His Coat of Many

Colors—the trusted advisor to the wise Pharaoh of the Book of Genesis in the Old Testament.

Hers was not a superstitious nature, but considering the importance she attached to the significance of names, in later years she must have wondered if Grandfather's unexpected slip had not jeopardized her teachings in the case of Herbert, who developed a predilection for the pubs and an aversion to the church.

Indeed, she even informed me of the origin of my name, something I was unaware of and, as it turned out, would have preferred not to know. During her pregnancy Mother was reading a novel whose heroine was named Beatrice. Grandmother had thought this name an unfortunate choice for me since the heroine had committed suicide. I was left to digest that unsettling news. In the working-class Oldtown it was too much to hope that the literary inspiration for my name had come from Shakespeare's witty and clever Beatrice in *Much Ado about Nothing* or Dante's Beatrice in *Vita Nuova*.

But if her sons had failed to live up to her expectations or the names she had bestowed on them, Grandmother never admitted it. She only spoke of them with pride, of their handsome appearance and their popularity with women. Indeed, there were a surprising number of photos of the three eldest with girls on their arms. And I took careful note of her warning that the Morrows had the failing of being hot-headed.

Although Grandmother talked about her sons, family, relatives, friends and acquaintances from the old days in

Caledon, I have no clear impression of my grandfather's personality. In a family photograph he and Grandmother look happy and proud as they pose with their five young sons. She, pretty, smiling and content with her family, sits on one side of the young boys, while he, a man with piercing, deep-set eyes below bushy eyebrows and an even bushier mustache, sits on the other.

He must have been a loyal Orangeman because tucked in the family Bible is a copy of Ulster's Solemn League and Covenant signed by William John Morrow on September 28, 1912. Almost a quarter of a million Protestant Ulstermen signed this document in Belfast City Hall in protest against Home Rule for Ireland and as a pledge to fight for the independence of Ulster should the Home Rule Bill be passed by the British Parliament.

Granny Morrow was meticulous in keeping records of her family, recording births, marriages and deaths in the family Bible, even preserving the page from her parents' Bible where the Westermans' important dates were listed. Surprising, then, is the lack of information about Grandfather, when he was born and when he died. But many Irish, including my mother, were unsure of their dates of birth. No importance was attached to them. Birthdays were not celebrated in poorer families, and until the days of government pensions and higher education for the working classes, birth certificates or proof of age was unnecessary.

Unfortunately, the page recording Grandfather's death is missing, discovered by my brother when he inherited Granny's

Bible. But I have the impression that Grandfather was about sixty-five years old when he died, making him approximately ten years older than his wife. It made an indelible impression on me as a child to hear he had died of hiccups, their cause completely forgotten.

After his death Granny tried unsuccessfully to maintain the butcher's shop with my father in charge. But he was only twenty, too young for so much responsibility and for the sudden freedom after a strict upbringing. The shop was eventually sold, and Father moved to Cookstown to work.

Accompanied by her three youngest sons, Herbie, Lewie and Joe, Granny followed soon afterwards. A few years earlier Harold had emigrated to Queensland on the Australian government's assisted passage program, repaying his fare by working in the sugar cane fields for a couple of years before establishing a successful dairy business in Adelaide.

Granny's opinion of Cookstown was not favorable. However, her life in Cookstown was very different from that in Caledon. She had lived in Caledon for over thirty years, the respected wife of a shopkeeper, surrounded by friends and relatives, an upstanding member of the Presbyterian Church, singing in its choir. It was there she had spent her happiest years, raised her children, buried her father and her husband.

Moreover, Caledon was a village of a few hundred people compared to Cookstown, a thriving market town with a population of roughly five thousand. She did not care for its people, thinking them shallow and cold. Not surprisingly, she never made any friends in Cookstown, keeping to herself and her family.

Equally devastating was her opinion of its women— a fast lot, blamed for snaring her sons the moment they set foot in the town. That they were grown men of marriageable age was not mentioned. After all, Father was almost thirty when he married Mother, who had just turned twenty, and Joe was twenty-six when he married Alice, several years his junior. Compared to her generation, they had married younger, but it was hardly the cradle snatching she implied. Taken aback by her remarks, I quickly cast my mind over the aunts and my mother, but none appeared the temptress Grandmother accused them of being.

But like many mothers, she was probably reluctant to lose control of her sons, to be dethroned in their affections. She need not have worried. All of them had the highest regard for her, and Granny was held up as a paragon to their wives.

When Granny first moved to Cookstown, she lived at Sandhurst, a terrace of small brick houses with front gardens and railings on the Moneymore Road, at the edge of the town. However, when Lewie married, she was forced to move to more modest surroundings, still located on the Moneymore Road, only a stone's throw from three of her sons: Stanley, Lewie and Joe.

But Grandmother did not compromise her standards. Having nothing in common with the neighbors, she went about her business, limiting her contact with them to a polite "Good morning" or an acknowledgment of the state of the weather.

Before long a flower border edged the back of the house. Then a vegetable garden was cultivated with the help of her sons. A flower garden was added with old-fashioned perennials— red-hot pokers, snapdragons, pansies, snowdrops—flowers for every season, a small lawn and a summer seat. She loved gardening, and plants thrived under her green thumb. Most of her flowers came from "slips," pieces from other people's plants. Once her housework was taken care of, she spent many a pleasant afternoon working there. On long summer evenings, she relaxed with her sons while grandchildren played on the grass.

Inside, the house gleamed and order reigned. A large, dark green dresser with its sparkling dishes and neatly arranged drawers occupied one wall of the kitchen. In front of the window stood a wooden table, scrubbed white and surrounded by a few straight chairs. Beside the range a small armchair provided a respite from work, and a large, black clock ticked solemnly on the wall.

Every afternoon after dinner, the main meal, eaten in the middle of the day, Granny moved the fire from the kitchen range to the parlor fireplace. This, in itself, was an extraordinary event in the Oldtown, where parlors sat unused, cold and damp, while families crowded into cramped kitchens.

Her parlor was warm and cozy, a contrast to the starkness and workaday atmosphere of the kitchen. Granny's armchair waited beside the fireplace, her harmonium against one wall. A small, mahogany gate-leg table was placed below the window with its lace curtains. Ornaments and family photographs decorated the mantelpiece and furniture. And out of reach for little hands was a candy dish on top of the bookcase. Grandmother and Grandfather, photographed on their wedding day, surveyed the scene from their ornate Victorian frames.

It was to the tranquility of Granny's parlor that I escaped, away from the turmoil and bedlam of brothers and sisters at home, to do my homework or to enjoy her companionship. It was here I sat for hours by the fireside, drinking in her stories.

Hers was the only house where the past was ever mentioned. Mother hated to talk about the past, and one never thought of questioning Granny Hamilton about such topics. Indeed, one didn't have conversations with Granny Hamilton. It was always hurry, scurry. Nor did she have much time for children or empathy with them. Granny Morrow, on the other hand, treated children as she treated adults.

For a number of years she received the grandchildren on Wednesday afternoons during the summer holidays and at Christmas. At half-past two the aunts deposited the cousins neatly dressed, faces scrubbed, hair combed. As we sat around the parlor fire, Granny read stories or played games. We gave little concerts modeled on those we had seen in church halls. In those pre-TV days, variety shows or concerts were a popular form of entertainment.

Preparations for our little plays and skits in which brother Harold, cousin Valerie and I played the leading roles, took place in the kitchen. While Granny and the younger cousins sat expectantly waiting, we made our dramatic entrance into the parlor through the heavy curtain which hung over the door in winter to keep out the draughts.

We gathered round the harmonium as she accompanied our high, childish voices in singing hymns and songs. One Christmas our carol singing was interrupted by loud knocking on the door. It was the rent-collector. As we crowded round Granny at the door, he expressed his amazement. He had assumed the beautiful singing was coming from the wireless.

The afternoons ended with tea: home-baked bread and blackcurrant or gooseberry jam, buns or a piece of rhubarb pie made with rhubarb from her garden. Everyone ate politely, seated around the kitchen table, no grabbing or shouting. Only good behavior and manners were tolerated at Granny Morrow's, and those who misbehaved or disobeyed were not welcomed back.

The Wednesday afternoons came to an end when the grandchildren became too numerous for her small house. Instead we dropped by in the evenings. I enjoyed those evenings, especially as I got older and often went alone or accompanied by one of my younger siblings.

Granny had games, board games she loved to play. Her favorite word game was Lexicon, a precursor of Scrabble. She took it seriously, and though a little assistance was given to the younger fry, it was played competitively and no rules were bent for age. The uncles and cousins, whom we often encountered there, joined in, and many a winter's evening was spent around the kitchen table searching for odd words, the dictionary consulted when a controversy occurred. Granny herself had a large vocabulary and regularly did the crossword puzzles from the newspaper.

Reluctantly she played Checkers and Dominoes with us, much preferring an older, more difficult game related to Chess. It was impossible to beat her at these games, and she was not of the generation that thought children's self-esteem depended on letting them win. Cards, other than those of the Old Maid variety, were not permitted in this strict Presbyterian household.

Because the Sabbath was strictly observed, hymn-singing replaced games on Sunday evenings. Lewis was a fine tenor, Joe could hold a tune and Father also had a good singing voice. When or where Granny had learned to read music and play the harmonium, I never knew. It was yet another of her remarkable accomplishments and talents.

Considering her limited formal education and the working class environment in which she lived, she was exceedingly well read. Her reading habits and interests were reflected in the contents of the bookcase. Religious books were to the fore: *The Pilgrim's Progress* with its terrifying engravings of the Pilgrim's journey, protected by crisp, crinkly tissue paper pages; *The Compendium and Concordance* for serious Bible study; a Bible for daily reading; a hymn book complete with music; and a dictionary.

Her library books and light reading, occupying another shelf, were the novels of J.B. Priestley, George Eliot, Georges Sand, the Brontes, Charles Dickens and Thomas Hardy. Children's books also had their place: Bible stories and fairy tales she had read to her sons and then to her grandchildren. On the bottom shelf the heavy, ornate family Bible and photograph album were stored. As I grew older, I spent many hours perusing these books while she read, crocheted or knitted.

Grandmother was an excellent needlewoman, equally skilled in knitting, crocheting, and embroidery, never using a pattern but creating her own. Her tablecloths, traycloths and pillowcases made from scraps of linen, were edged with her beautiful white lace and drawn-work embroidery. Lace doilies adorned the tables and chair backs. White lace gloves were crocheted for summer, and lace collars for the necks of her dresses and sweaters.

Religion was an important part of her life. Originally Methodist, married into the Presbyterians, she was an ardent churchgoer. Her children had been brought up strictly in accordance with her religious and Victorian principles. Her adult sons were expected to attend church regularly and to instill this habit in their children. Dutifully, as Father had done, we went to Sunday school and church every Sunday morning and often to church again at night. We accompanied Granny Morrow to special services at our own church and the Methodist church.

I spent many Sunday afternoons studying the Bible with her at the little table in her parlor. Under her guidance

I consulted the *Concordance* and *Bible*, searching for answers to questions in the Sunday school magazine. Then, under her critical eye I transcribed them in my best handwriting, in ink, with a straight-nibbed pen, and mailed them off in the hope of a prize.

When Harold and I accompanied her on holiday to Great-aunt Mary Jane's thatched cottage in the country at Curlough, saying our prayers was strictly enforced. At home prayers were also part of the nightly ritual, but if the weather was cold, we raced through the Lord's Prayer, quickly asked God for a few blessings and jumped into bed.

This was not a day and age when intimacy and affection were exhibited by adults to children. We were unaccustomed to seeing Granny in this intimate setting where we shared sleeping quarters and were somewhat intimidated by her. Ours was a puritanical society, and, strange as it may seem nowadays, children rarely saw adults in their nightwear and certainly never in their underwear.

Ready for bed in her long, white flannel nightgown, her waist-length, white hair unloosed from its bun, Granny seemed different, taller. Physically she was very small, barely five feet. Only as a teenager towering over her as we walked home from church together, did I ever think of her as small.

Mother, who was also small but inclined to be plump, admired Granny's "wee, neat figure." Everything about Grandmother was neat: her appearance, her house, her habits. Whether doing her chores, going shopping or reading quietly

by the fire, she was always immaculate. Her clothes were conservative, typical of the days when rules of dress were strictly
followed. On Sundays she wore a black dress, the bodice taste-
fully trimmed with a narrow, white ruffle and fastened at the
neck with a brooch. At other times it was a wool skirt and
hand-knitted sweater or maybe a blouse or a dress in summer,
but always in black or gray.

Still somewhat vain about her appearance, she occasionally primped her white hair in little waves to give it more full-
ness, setting off her fine features. Every morning she washed
her face in cold water, good for the skin, she said, and she had
beautiful skin, even as an old lady.

Her habits were as orderly as her appearance. Twice a
week, donning her black coat and hat, she set off with a pur-
poseful step down the town to collect her pension, change her
library books or do her shopping. Over one arm hung a rectangular, brown wicker basket containing her library books, on
the other arm an umbrella or handbag. On Sundays the basket
was replaced by a Bible and hymn book.

Her appearance and her house reflected her temperament and personality: organized, competent, quiet and calm.
Hers were not the untidy, easy-going habits of the Irish, nor had
she the fiery, impulsive nature of the Morrows. Composed and
self-possessed, she appeared every inch a lady, a term not normally applied to the working-class inhabitants of the Oldtown.

Not riddled by self-doubt, she never wallowed in
depression or threw up her hands in despair but resolutely and

cheerfully met the challenges of life. She was a clever, intelligent woman who excelled at everything she did, as interested in being a frugal housekeeper as reading good literature. She enjoyed using her mind, seeking the only intellectual outlets available to her in crosswords, games and literature.

Her leisure time was spent in creative, worthwhile pursuits, for she preferred her own company to gossip with the neighbors. She conveyed a sense of superiority by her attitude, her accomplishments, her aloofness to neighbors and acquaintances—a superiority she transferred to me. I felt Granny was special and the Morrows were special. Secure in her religious beliefs, which took care of the next life, she was content with this one and her place in it. Unfortunately, she thought we should be content with our place in society as well.

But the world was changing. The period after World War II was a time of great social change. For the first time people like ourselves had the chance to continue our education beyond the age of fourteen. Grandmother made it very plain she disapproved of Mother's sending Harold and me to the Rainey School in Magherafelt, a school with a reputation for academic excellence, when there was a perfectly adequate high school in Cookstown. If Cookstown High School was good enough for the children of her wealthy landlord, it should have been good enough for us.

Imagine her reaction when I went to Queen's University, followed by Harold two years later. I was the first Morrow ever to attend high school, and now Mother had the audacity to send me to the university. To Grandmother higher learning was reserved for the education of Presbyterian ministers and the upper classes. Once more we had overstepped our place in society. Ironically, I had earned that scholarship, studying my advanced math by the light of the oil lamp in her parlor.

Grandmother's sense of duty never failed even when it was almost too much for her. In the summer of 1947 or '48 an epidemic of polio swept through Northern Ireland. Uncle Lewie's wife Mabel, pregnant at the time, was one of its random victims. She and the baby died in childbirth, leaving three young children. Grandmother, at the age of seventy-five, packed her bags, closed her house, and went off to Downpatrick to look after the newly orphaned family until Lewie remarried. I missed her terribly, and it was a great relief when Granny returned a year later.

Harold and I were the privileged grandchildren who accompanied Granny Morrow on her family visits. Just as we had traveled with her to visit Great-aunt Mary Jane, her in-laws and friends around Caledon, we now went along with her to visit Lewie and his new wife in Downpatrick.

Blessed with good health, mentally and physically active, Granny was a wonderful example of growing old gracefully. Still living alone in her eighties, self-reliant and independent to a fault, she climbed on a stool to paint, became dizzy and fell. After that she was unable to live alone. Uncle Lewie returned the favor she had done him nearly ten years earlier, and, until her death not long afterwards, she lived with him in Magherafelt, where he now was manager of the gasworks.

She died in September 1955 at the start of my third year at Queen's University. Much to the annoyance of my father, I was unable to attend her funeral, which coincided with an important examination. So I never said my final farewell to the grandmother who had meant so much to me.

For years I had a recurring dream in which I see her house on the Moneymore Road, hushed now, the door ajar to allow the family to enter without knocking. Inside, Granny lies motionless on the sofa in the parlor. She is very ill. Her white hair frames her face; she is dressed in her black Sunday dress with the white ruffle at the neck. There is no sound. I walk past her house. I look through the window, but I never go in.

I had never visited her grave, as her sons and grandsons had taken her back to Caledon to bury her beside her husband in the little graveyard of the Presbyterian church she had attended so faithfully every Sunday. But in the summer of 1996 I went back to Caledon for the first time since my childhood visits with Granny nearly fifty years earlier.

I found a village bypassed in time, a village of gray stone, a village with its castle boarded up, the Carleton Arms Hotel closed and the weighing machine, used in the days of the railroad, enclosed behind a wrought iron fence, an antique now. I went into the grocery shop and asked directions to the grave-yard. The proprietor took me into her house adjoining the shop and there, lining the walls of the hallway, were the old black and white photos of Caledon, in the snow, with its railroad, the old photos I recognized from Granny's album.

I walked around the little graveyard, gazing at the gray stone church with its lofty spire, searching for her grave. "Under the big tree," my brother had said. "There is no headstone."

I stood there silently, remembering the days and evenings spent in her company, acknowledging the qualities I had inherited from her and grateful for the influence she had been on my life.

A Death in the Family

I will lift up mine eyes unto the hills,
from whence doth come mine aid.
—*Psalm 121:1*

Iflung open the bedroom window and took a deep breath. Lines of washing whipped back and forth in the stiff breeze coming off Slieve Gallion, the mountain that looked down on our street. It was Monday when every housewife did her weekly wash. But this Monday no washing hung from our line; no sweaters dried on the hawthorn hedge between our garden and our neighbor's next door. My father had died early that morning.

Although my father was scheduled for surgery, Mother had insisted I stick to my plans and visit my friend Olive for a few days during the Easter holidays.

"Go on. Stop worrying. There's nothing you can do. Everything will be all right now that he is going into the hospital. If he gets any worse, I'll phone you."

But early that Monday morning in March 1957, Olive's mother had knocked on the bedroom door to say, "Bea, get up. Your mother just phoned."

I jumped out of bed panic-stricken. Something had gone drastically wrong. My mother was not one for false alarms. Why had Mrs. Hutchinson not let me talk to her?

An hour later Olive parked the car in front of our little row house. There was no sign of life. The blinds were drawn,

closed like the eyes of the dead, as was the custom. My sister
Bertha opened the front door in response to my frantic knocking. Mother followed a few steps behind, her dark eyes sunk
deeper than ever in her sallow face.

"You know," her eyes said.

I nodded, unable to speak, tears running down my face,
and threw my arms round her neck. All the way home I had
worried about my mother, my brothers and sisters, all seven
younger than I. To think I hadn't been home when they needed
me. My poor mother. Was there no end to her troubles? She
was constantly being tested in the fire but so far had never bent.

In the backyard I found Harold, my oldest brother,
cleaning out the byre. No matter what calamity occurred in
our lives, the animals had to be looked after, but today it was
also his way of keeping calm.

"What happened last night?" I asked him.

"At seven o'clock Doctor Elliott phoned Mrs. Allen to
say Father's operation was a success. Then about midnight a
knock came to the door. It was Mrs. Allen back again to say
the doctors were doing all they could, but Father seemed to
have given up the will to live, and would Mother come to the
hospital at once. Uncle Joe went with her."

If that's not typical of Father to give up, I thought. He
never had any backbone. All the anger and resentment I had
felt for him during my teenage years came crowding in on me,
followed by feelings of guilt because we had often dismissed his
complaints as those of a hypochondriac.

"I was milking the cows this morning when Mother came home from the hospital," Harold continued, glad to have somebody to confide in. "Mother appeared at the byre door and said, 'Your father's dead.'"

"That's all?" I asked. "Was she crying?" Mother rarely cried.

Harold shook his head. "I asked her what we were going to do, and she just quietly said, 'We'll manage, we'll manage somehow.' and went into the house."

But how, how would we manage? That thought had raged through my mind from the moment I had learned of Father's death. Not quite twenty years old, I was the oldest of the eight children he had left. Harold was a year-and-a-half younger, and the baby was only nine months old. What would we live on? Nobody was working. Harold and I were at University. Would we have to give up our scholarships and go to work?

It would break my mother's heart if we had to quit our studies, but I knew Mother would receive only a miserly pension because Father was in arrears with his payments to the government and had no insurance. Once again he had left us in the lurch. Our lives had always been in constant turmoil because of his impetuous, impractical nature, his quick temper and his drinking habit.

I felt like screaming at the cows, "The drinking days are over, and you'll be the next to go," and immediately regretted it. It wasn't their fault. "Be kind to dumb animals" was one of Father's tenets; what a shame he hadn't extended it to his family.

For a man with a weakness for drink, my father had the worst possible job. As a small-time cattle-dealer, he went to fairs and markets all over the North of Ireland. Unfortunately, it was the custom to repair to the nearest pub to seal the sale of a bullock or a heifer.

For the two years before his death Father had not been drinking, but we never knew the day or hour he would start again. All it took was one drink. I realized Father walked a tightrope each day. Just a stroll down Cookstown's mile-long main street with its eighteen pubs was an exercise in willpower and abstention for a recovering alcoholic.

Memories came crowding in on me as I looked around the backyard where he had built hen houses and cattle sheds, and where I, too, had had to work under his impatient regime. Suddenly one of the cows let out a long, low bellow and I jumped. Well, at least now there'll be no more children, I thought. That will be one blessing.

Mother's goal in life was to educate her children so that they would have a better life than she. "An education is easily carried," she often advised me when we sat up late at night, drinking tea, chatting and knitting by the fireside after everyone else had gone to bed. And I saw myself stepping out into the world, swinging my invisible briefcase by my side.

Education was the only way to escape the confines of the working class and break the pattern of men spending their hard-earned money in pubs on Saturday nights while their families barely scraped a living. In spite of her hard existence and over my father's objections Mother sacrificed and struggled, somehow finding enough money so that we could continue to go to school after the age of fourteen.

But our immediate challenge for the next two days was to cope with the funeral and the wake. After that we would face the problem of no money and how we were going to manage. Father had left six pounds sterling, a few cattle and hens.

From the moment Father's body was brought home from the hospital that Monday afternoon and laid out in the parlor, I felt as if his presence pervaded the entire house. The downstairs had only three small rooms; a parlor, kitchen and scullery; and the upstairs consisted of three bedrooms and a bathroom. There was nowhere, other than the crowded kitchen, to receive the neighbors and relatives, who stopped by to offer their condolences. The newspaper had stated "House Private," partly for that reason, but many came anyway.

Every time I went down the narrow hall to answer the front door, I had to pass the parlor. Some people stepped into the hall but stayed only a few minutes to shake my mother's hand or to say to one of us, "Tell your mother I'm sorry for her trouble." But to others Mother, her face gray and taut from shock and sleepless nights, had to recount endlessly the story of her husband's illness and death.

Before the visitors left, many requested to see Father's body. When it was my turn to see them out, I steeled myself and looked the other way as I pointed them to the parlor door. I leaned against the wall, while I waited for them to come out, and stared at my reflection in the hall mirror. I asked myself, when are you going to have the courage to go and do the same? Would I add to my burden of guilt if I allowed him to be buried without showing him that difficult sign of respect. Unlike Mother he had always placed great importance on the rituals and customs connected with burying the dead. She believed in doing for the living.

"The country ones are the devil for looking at dead bodies," was Mother's dry comment, and Father knew a lot of country ones because of buying and selling cattle. Mother refused to go near the parlor, but then she hated funerals and never partook of invitations to view the dead. She never understood people who went to wakes and declared, "Ah, doesn't he make a lovely corpse." Or those who dwelt on the expressions of the dead person's face, mouthing platitudes: "He has such a peaceful expression." What did they hope to see?

On the night before the funeral, after I had closed the door on the last caller, I went back to the kitchen. As we sat around the fire having a cup of tea, discussing the funeral arrangements, I said to Harold and Bertha, "Don't you think we should go and pay our last respects to Father tomorrow?"

Harold gave me a withering look and went off to bed. He would have to help carry his father's coffin, and Noel and Derek, the younger boys, would walk behind the hearse. At that time it was the custom in Northern Ireland for women and young children to stay at home and not to attend the funeral service in church or go to the cemetery, so Bertha, Mother and I would be spared that ordeal. Still, it bothered me to think nobody in the family would go near the parlor.

"You must be joking," Bertha declared. "I think not, indeed. After all he did to us."

Although I had often wished for my father's death, the sudden nature of it had lifted the lid on many memories, good and bad, that I had suppressed. When we were young, Father often took us for long Sunday afternoon walks while he examined sheep and cattle belonging to the local farmers. We wandered freely through their fields, gathering wildflowers as we went. In springtime he reached up to get us bunches of silvery catkins from the willows or lambs' tails that dangled from the birch trees.

We searched the moist, shady banks of sheughs and ditches to find primroses, violets and bluebells. Because it was Sunday, Mother would be waiting for us with tea already laid out on the white linen tablecloth. Soon our flowers would brighten and perfume the kitchen from the white bowl with the blue rim on the windowsill.

"Who would like to get up early in the morning and gather mushrooms?" Father asked from time to time. "I noticed a good crop in the field this morning when I went to fetch the cows."

Noel, who was an early riser like Father, always volunteered, but there was usually silence from the rest of the family.

Bertha and Derek were not nature lovers. "I'll come," I said because Father looked disappointed that few shared his enthusiasm to go foraging through the dew. On our return Father insisted on mushrooms on toast for breakfast. I would have preferred something less pungent, but Mother scoffed so much at the whole idea that I cooked and ate them for his sake. It had been a long time since I remembered anything good about my father.

Shortly before the funeral, I escaped upstairs. I needed a few minutes alone; I felt stifled in the crowded, little house full of despair and people. If only I could get away from the pitying voices of the neighbors and the smug advice of the uncles.

"Poor Mrs. Morrow … left like that. Eight of them, did you say?"

"Aye, and the youngest only nine months old."

I had bristled when I overheard Uncle Joe say to Mother, "Take the two big ones out of college. Put them to work."

From the bedroom above the kitchen I could hear the mumble of women's voices and the front door opening and closing. Harold knocked on the door to say, "You'd better get yourself tidied up. The men are beginning to gather."

The funeral, which was at two o'clock, started from the house. It would be a relief when it was over. Trying to appear calm and composed for Mother's sake and for the sake of the younger children was not easy. My five-year-old sister kept asking, "Where's Daddy?"

It was hard to believe he would never be back. When my brother and uncles carried him out in his coffin this afternoon, it would be forever. There would be no more reason to dread his return, or listen for his footsteps coming down the entry when I was washing dishes or peeling potatoes in the scullery, or examine his face as he passed the window. I could read his moods as easily as he could predict the weather from glancing up at the mountain—winter or summer, cold and wet; or sunny and bright.

I went into my parents' bedroom, which looked out on the street. Clumps of men dressed in their Sunday suits stood talking quietly together, waiting for the hearse to arrive. Father would have been pleased there was such a big turnout. Farmers and cattle dealers, relatives, men from the church and neighbors, they were all there. I wondered if any publicans were among them, or if they bothered to attend the funerals of their former customers. What about his drinking companions? Where were they?

My parents' wedding photo hung above their bed. Father was tall and blond, Mother short and dark, opposites in looks as well as personality. Mother was only twenty that day, the same age as I. I sighed, determined not to cry. Bertha came running up the stairs with the baby. "Bea, what are you doing? You've got to come down. Here, put the baby to bed; it's time for his nap." I tucked the baby into his crib. I kissed him and thought how strange, unlike me, he will never know his father. Later on, when he is old enough, I will tell him about the hard times, but I will also tell him about the primroses, bluebells and mushrooms and how Father loved animals.

I went back to my room with its view of the gardens and the mountain. Although Slieve Gallion looked so close, it was seven miles of steep, rough, dirt roads to Lough Fea and the Bronze Age stone circles. Seven rows of stone circles and burial cairns were evidence that people had lived in the Sperrin Mountains for over 5,000 years. I wished I were there. Among the heather and whins I always felt their comforting, ancestral presence around me as if their spirits had entered into the rocks and stones, into the lakes of the mountain.

I glanced down at the neighbors' lines of washing. Mother would be sorry to miss such a good drying day. The neighbors must be spring-cleaning. Sheets and blankets billowed on the lines like sails, flapped like white flags of surrender. I heaved a sigh of relief. With Mother there would be no surrender.

"What's it all about?" Mother often queried as we bent over the washtub on Monday mornings, working in tandem. I scrubbed the clothes on the washboard while she wrung them out, the muscles in her strong arms, relaxing and tightening as she twisted the heavy, wet towels and sheets.

"There's nothing for it but to carry on, keep going," Mother would conclude, as we bent over the tub once again, plunging our arms in up to the elbows in soap suds and water. Her question came back to me. "What's it all about?"

With Mother we would survive. We had been through tough times before. She would not allow our lives to be torn apart, she never had.

As I closed the window, I noticed a shaft of sunlight had pierced the gray-rimmed clouds, illuminating a field on the side of the mountain and painting it gold. Suddenly my reverie was interrupted by someone calling to me from the bottom of the stairs. It was my aunt's voice. "Bea, do you want to see your father before they close the coffin?" Before answering, I took a deep breath. "Yes. Yes, I do. Tell them to wait a minute."

I felt a sudden sense of freedom as if a burden had been lifted. Before returning to University (I would find a way to go back), I would bicycle up to Slieve Gallion to visit those ancient stone circles, which were standing tall and erect again, bearing witness once more to the mystery of life, after having been buried for centuries beneath layers of peat. Every Easter, when we were young, Harold and I had gone to the mountain with Father to gather the prickly whins' yellow blossoms in order to dye our eggs.

It was Easter and the whins were in bloom.

Beaghmore Stone Circles

Stones of Time

The past echoes from monuments of stones
On Ireland's mountains, plains and shores
Its mystery chiseled in limestone and granite.

Who wrought these megaliths and cairns,
Dolmens and mighty passage tombs?
The past echoes from monuments of stones.

What does the Janus figure meditate
Among hawthorns, nettles and Christian gravestones?
Its mystery chiseled in limestone and granite.

What gods were worshiped in sacrifices
At stone circles aligned to the summer solstice?
The past echoes from monuments of stones.

Man leaves his funereal markers,
Bold evidence of his ephemeral passage,
Hieroglyphics remain on the stones
Their mystery chiseled in limestone and granite.

Mother as a Child

Her sister Evelynn

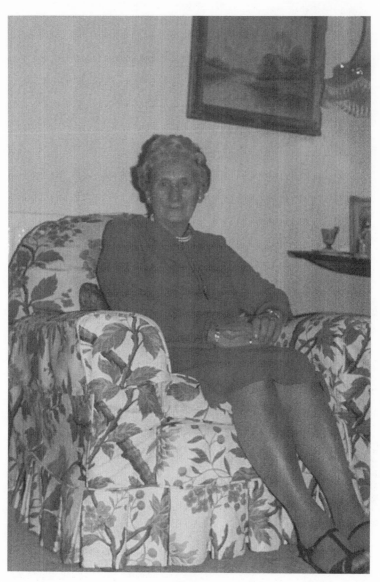

Mother

Mother

Remember me
whispers the dust.
—Peter Huchel

How could I forget her? She was the keystone of our existence. We had everything money couldn't buy: poverty, uncertainty, fear, and Mother. Home wasn't home, if she wasn't in it.

"Where's your mother?" were Father's first words, if he didn't set eyes on her the minute he pushed open the back door. One of us immediately volunteered to find her. The kitchen was her domain, and while Father was living, she rarely strayed far from it. Unless she was downtown shopping, she was usually in the garden either hanging out clothes or taking them in. Occasionally she could be found chatting to Mrs. Mason next door, but unlike her mother, she didn't gossip around the neighbors.

It was not until her younger sister married that my mother ever had a holiday or a break from the responsibilities that increased year by year, child by child. I dreaded her going, her week or few days at Aunt Evelynn's, for then I was left to take her place and look after my father and the children. It became a yearly habit, and the only one who accompanied her on the bus to Omagh was the current baby; first Clifford, then Marcella and finally Trevor.

I would have preferred it if she had taken Father with her and left the baby with me. Babies I knew how to take care of, but he was another matter. Not only was he difficult to live with, but he expected the house to run as smoothly as if she were at the helm; I was only thirteen or fourteen when these annual pilgrimages began. As soon as the summer holidays started, I inquired when she was going. I wanted to get the ordeal over and not waste the summer worrying about it.

She would vacillate, just as she would years later when she came to visit me, about whether she would go or not, but go she always did. Somehow I survived my father's short temper and his unrealistic expectations, while coping with five or six children, but not my mother's lack of consideration. If I dreaded her leaving, I couldn't wait for her return. That day I would clean and tidy the house, scrub the children's faces once again and set off with the little ones to meet the one and only bus coming from Omagh. Inevitably she didn't get off it. Then we trudged home, a dejected group, with anger and resentment filling my heart.

On the rare occasions she wasn't at home, and before I was old enough to take care of the others after school, we went to Granny Hamilton's. She lived just up the hill from us, but was always busy with her sewing and hadn't much patience with children. When we asked for something to eat, she cut thick slices of loaf bread, spread them with homemade damson, gooseberry, blackcurrant or rhubarb jam, mumbling, "You Morrow scrubs, does your mother never feed you?" If Mother was later than usual, we stood outside on the street anxiously watching for her to come over the Oldtown Hill with her basket and sometimes a treat.

When Derek was born, the fifth and last child to be delivered at home, I was eight, and remember looking wistfully down the street to our house, accompanied by the other three, forbidden to go home.

I begrudged my mother her every outing, no matter how short or how necessary, while my father was alive. Even when she lingered in the garden, cutting flowers after hanging out clothes, it annoyed me, for I was impatient to finish the housework. Only then would I be released to follow my own pursuits, find somewhere quiet to read, or play with my cousin and brothers. It was not until I was a mother myself that I understood her need for a few quiet moments to herself, and her need to surround herself with what beauty she could find. Unlike Granny Morrow who believed flowers should be left in the garden, Mother brought them into the house where we could smell and enjoy them as we went about our daily tasks.

As the oldest of her eight children and, being a girl, I was expected to work side by side with her when I wasn't at school. Capable and responsible though I was from an early age, I hated housework. To me it seemed such a waste of time to sweep and clean the house when it would be just as bad the next day. This was not Mother's philosophy. Moreover, she was a perfectionist whose motto still rings in my head: "If a job is worth doing, it's worth doing right." It was instilled in me the hard way, by my redoing sloppy work.

Mother had enough energy for two people and believed we should have the same enthusiasm as she had for tackling whatever job needed doing. If I dared complain of being tired, she gave me one of her disgusted looks, followed by "Tired at your age! A change is as good as a rest." The words "tired" and "rest" were not part of her working vocabulary and were not permitted in ours.

I loved to read and often tried to sneak in a few pages while I made beds or cleaned bedrooms. Soon I would be recalled to the real world by Mother's voice from the bottom of the stairs, "What's taking so long up there?"

It was hard to outwit her. If I sat down with a book, a baby or a piece of knitting landed in my lap, but I became adept at handling each of these tasks while reading . I propped the book on the arm of the sofa, which was fairly high, and cradled the baby on my opposite arm to give it its bottle. Knitting while reading was more difficult. Like many people we knitted all our sweaters, mittens, scarves, as well as socks for my father and the boys. There was always some garment in urgent need of a few rows "while you are doing nothing." Unless it was a complicated pattern or an intricate stitch, I could knit without looking until I got to the end of a row, drag my reluctant eyes from the book propped once again on the arm of the sofa, turn the garment quickly around, start the new row, and return hurriedly to the book for another few moments of stolen pleasure.

If a recipe or a knitting pattern pleased Mother, it became part of our repertoire, of which the most striking example was the family uniform. Originally she had knitted matching sweaters for Harold and me when we were three and four years old. A gray-flannel pleated skirt or short pants, made by Granny Hamilton, complemented these short-sleeved gray sweaters with rainbow stripes. The handing down and production of these garments went on for twenty years, for there was almost a twenty-year difference between me and my youngest brother, Trevor. Our family of little blonde children like steps of stairs was unmistakable when it went on the Sunday School excursion dressed in these matching outfits.

Maybe it was our first mark of distinction. Later she was so proud when she met people and they referred to her children as "The Clever Morrows." And so she should have been, for she deserved the praise. Against my father's wishes and at great sacrifice to herself, especially after his death, she had done everything possible to see that we had an education, after having observed the difference it had made in her younger sister's life.

Her aim and ambition was that we would have the opportunity for a better life than she had. She was determined we would get out of our working class environment. The same rigorous standards Mother applied to household tasks and the formation of our characters were applied to our performance at school.

When Harold and I were in primary school, she supervised our homework. She listened to our spellings and tables, checked our sums and writing, which were done in pencil first, then entered in our notebooks in ink with a straight-nibbed pen. Many a tear was shed as she ripped out a page because of inkblots or mistakes. Our cries that the teacher did not allow us to tear out pages went unheeded.

Perfect attendance and perfect marks were our primary goals. I loved school and enjoyed learning, but it was hard to meet her demands of never being lower than third in any examination. Even though she needed my help as the family increased, I was never asked to do housework when I had home-work to do.

I went to a high school whose headmaster had the same philosophy as Mother. To prevent me from having a free period three times a week, he insisted I take Domestic Science for two years, as if I needed more instruction in running a house. But it did have one immediate benefit; I became the pastry expert in the family. After years of perfect attendance at church on Sundays, for attendance at Sunday School and church was as rigidly enforced as at secular school, I was sometimes permitted to stay home and make steak and kidney pie for Sunday dinner.

Sunday dinner was a special event during the week: the white linen tablecloth was brought out, we had dessert, and Granny Morrow joined us. Mother never went to church on Sunday mornings, for dinner had to be ready the moment the churchgoers burst through the front door. Timing was critical, but our Reverend Morrison could usually be relied on to keep his sermon short. Occasionally the family was late.

"What's keeping them?" she'd inquire, before remembering it was the long-winded minister from Sandholes, Communion Sunday, or a baptism that day. I was dispatched to the front door to see if any churchgoers could be sighted cresting the Oldtown Hill. There were two Presbyterian churches in Cookstown; so I had to distinguish whether the passers-by, their heads replete with Christian teachings, and now scurrying home in anticipation of filling their stomachs, belonged to First or Third Cookstown.

Naturally there were times Mother and I disagreed. As a teenager I saw no reason why Harold couldn't iron his own white shirt before dashing off to a dance in one of the nearby towns. If I could compete with him in Advanced Math, he could learn to iron a shirt. I felt she was perpetuating the very habits in him that she was trying to break by giving us an equal education. I no longer felt I should take a back seat to the men in the family as she had been brought up to do.

Father, like most Irishmen of his generation, was accustomed to having his demands met instantly. When he took up cattle dealing in an effort to make a living, he had unpredictable and irregular hours. More often than not he arrived when the midday dinner was over, or had to rush off after some beast or bargain before we were due to eat our evening meal.

On such occasions, as soon as his footsteps were heard rounding the entry, the cry went up from Mother, "Get on the pan." It was made to appear that we were in the process of making his dinner or tea, as if we had extrasensory perception in the days before we even had a telephone. Father consumed a lot of our fast food, usually bacon and eggs.

On the morning of a local fair it was hustle and bustle from an early hour because my brothers accompanied him. I objected to being their handmaiden, attending the male members of the family hand and foot, but Mother insisted, "Just get on with it, get them out of here, and then we'll have peace and quiet." As soon as they had departed, the kettle was put on for a cup of tea, the fruitcake came out of hiding, for Mother had a sweet tooth. For a few minutes we indulged in a few pages of reading at opposite ends of the table.

Although she was a hard taskmaster, working with her was companionable as I got older, for she had a sense of humor and was interested in all our friends and activities. Like all the Hamilton women she was full of chat and expected us to be the same. Because I was shy and didn't easily engage in conversation with strangers, she used to reprimand me with the Irish expression, "Can't you put spake on yourself?" Actually I was embarrassed, when we traveled by bus and she struck up conversations with other passengers.

But if she was never lost for a topic of conversation and enjoyed nothing better than chatting round the fireside till late at night, she was reticent about her feelings and emotions. She refused to talk about the past, as if it were no longer of interest. She never shared any of the stories of her family, her youth or her meeting my father. I never dared ask, if she regretted marrying him.

Imagine my surprise when a few months before she died, she revealed we were related to the Bells, who lived four houses up the street from us. Tommy Bell was Granda Hamilton's half-brother. My cheeks burned to think I had delivered Tommy Bell's tea to his cobbler's shop for a shilling a week, and for years my family sat in the adjacent pew at church, and I had never known we were related.

It explained the seemingly incongruous friendship between him and Grandfather. Tommy Bell was an elder in the church, while Grandfather stayed in bed on Sundays, recovering from Saturday nights in the pub. Why were we never told this innocuous piece of information, when we lived on a street where everybody knew everybody else's business?

In the positive sense her negation of the past reflected her admirable quality of getting on with life and living in the present, instead of dreaming of what might have been. Although she never quoted scripture, she could have added Christ's words to her list of adages, "Let the dead bury their dead." "Do for the living," was one of the precepts by which she conducted herself, and we learned to appreciate the difference it made to us.

Thanks to her sense of responsibility, hard work and determination, we survived many difficult times while Father was still living. The year I turned thirteen, he was in and out of hospitals and spent months in bed. How she managed I don't know, but she plumbed her depths as she would do seven years later, when he died and left her with eight children and six pounds in the bank. Trevor was only nine months old and none of us were working, for Harold and I were still at Queen's University.

Her sister, who had no children of her own at the time, offered to adopt the baby, but Mother refused to separate us, "I'll keep them together." Father's brother offered his cheap advice, "Put the two big ones to work." But she hadn't sacrificed all those years to see her dreams collapse. I could hardly believe it when she sat Harold and me down after the funeral and said, "You'll stay where you are. We'll manage somehow."

Within one year her black hair had turned white, and although times were tough, she never looked back. With the dark undertow of my father's presence gone, the atmosphere in the house lightened, and we saw another side of Mother. After years of never going further than the clothesline, she joined in activities at church and became good at indoor and outdoor bowling. Once after spending the day in Belfast with me, she was running late for her match, so she jumped on one of the boy's bicycles, the one with the racing type handlebars and took off. Energy was never her problem; lack of money was. Finally she went to work, where, following in her father's footsteps she became the trade-union representative.

When I left Ireland and emigrated to Canada, every Sunday night she sat down and wrote to me, eight long pages relating all the family activities. Because of these letters I never lost touch and always remained close to her and the rest of the family. Although she missed each child terribly, when he or she left home, there were never any recriminations or pleading for us to stay nearby to help her. At first I came home every two or three years, and stayed a month or six weeks, for in the 1960s transatlantic travel was a major expense.

Our relationship entered a new phase, now that I was married and living overseas, and new experiences awaited her. As I moved around the world, I found a way for her to travel to see me. Nervous and apprehensive though she was about finding her way in major airports, she did visit me in Canada, Puerto Rico, Paris, Chicago, Connecticut and Brussels, and we spent holidays together in Corsica and Portugal.

If she and I shared the same straightforward character and blunt manner of speaking, we differed in appearance. I am tall and slim. She was short and stout. I am fair skinned, and in hot countries have to wear a hat and sit in the shade. Not so Mother with dark hair and olive complexion. She basked for hours in the sun, until I was afraid she would have sunstroke.

"You talk like a foreigner," she used to say to me when I gesticulated. I pointed out that it must be she who had the foreign blood, for her coloring was not typical of Northern Ireland. Maybe my grandmother's family, the McKinneys, I suggested, boasted an ancestor who had been shipwrecked off Galway during the days of the Spanish Armada in the sixteenth century. She gave short shift to such romantic ideas. "Have a bit of sense, Beatrice." It was a remark I often heard, when I aired my new-fangled notions.

Her second visit to the New World was shortly after my daughter was born in 1966, when she was fifty. As she and I sipped rum punches on the terrace of the Sheraton Hotel in San Juan, Puerto Rico, and looked out at the rustling palm trees and turquoise Caribbean, I remarked, "You were so tough when we were young."

"I had to be."

After a short illness and at the age of 75, she died on Thanksgiving Day, November 22, 1990, sitting in her armchair in front of the fire. Each year on that day I am reminded of what I have to be thankful for a mother, whose capacity for life and whose example of courage sustains me in difficult times. That same day the headline in the British newspapers announced "The End of an Era," referring to Prime Minister Margaret Thatcher's resignation. For her family it could also have served as the title of Mother's obituary.

The Mother

County Tyrone, N. Ireland

Cradled between a mountain
and a hill, our world
was a hard, parochial street
whose closed horizons
spiraled into the vortex,
the cyclops' eye of home.

There Mother forged
us in the fire
of hard work and schooling.
No dross, no excuses.

With the plangent sound
of her metal
still ringing in our ears,
we left our magus,
our forthright philosopher.

The past lies hammocked
in childhood memory.
We have lived
her dreams, dreamed
our dreams, as the future
unfolds in the diminishing
whorls of a seashell.

Thanksgiving Day

For my mother who died in N. Ireland on November 22, 1990

Through the steady procession of rain-
filled days and nights of murky water,
dark and bottomless as bogs of peat,
she struggled to breathe asthmatic air.

She, who loved the long light of northern
summer days, never wanted to let it go
by lighting lamps. *It's not dark yet.*
We can still see our faces.

Once she had visited the tropics where
brilliant light vibrated on a sapphire
ocean. *To think in all my years*
I'd seen only a blink of sun before.

But that last day alone with her dread
of slow dripping November,
there was only the faint hearth-
light to guide her on her way.

Bea at Deer Isle, Maine

Leaving Home

A traveler is ... to be reverenced ... going from toward,
it is the history of every one of us."

—Thoreau

If I could have turned back the clock, changed my mind about going to Canada that Sunday afternoon in early September 1960, I would have done so. But the die was cast; I had given up my job. My fiancé and a brand new job were waiting for me in Montreal. I had to go; it was too late.

Why did I want to change my mind at the last minute? My friend Connie was waiting to drive me to the airport, my two suitcases were packed, standing in the hall. I had planned consciously and unconsciously for this moment for a long time.

There had been no scenes, no weeping, nor recriminations from my mother about my decision to leave Ireland. But the moment of departure had finally come. The emotional floodgates had opened a short time earlier when I went to say good-bye to my grandmother. She was nearly eighty years old, and I didn't know when I would return.

Granda Hamilton never got up on Sundays, and Granny was upstairs resting on the bed beside him when I finally went up the Oldtown for the last time to see her.

"I'll probably never see you again," she said.

"No, no, I'll be back in a couple of years," I reassured her, trying to hold back the tears. By the time I returned home,

I was no longer in control. Those first tears had started to un-ravel the knot inside me.

Naturally my mother accompanied me to the airport, although I had tried to talk her out of it. I knew it would be difficult for me to say good-bye to her, and I wanted to get it over at home, and then compose myself for the journey ahead during the ride to the airport. As the car turned the Moneymore corner, I looked back at the house and through the tears could see my brothers and sisters, like steps of stairs, lined up at the front door waving good-bye.

At the airport my mother, who was not a demonstrative woman, cried and kissed me. It was the first time I ever remember her kissing me. The flight to Prestwick, Scotland was very short, even in 1960. I couldn't stop crying. I wished I could announce to the other passengers that I wasn't just going over to Scotland, a stone's throw away, but emigrating to Canada, that it wasn't the terror of the unknown that had reduced me to a blubbering mass, but the leave-taking.

During the long, thirteen-hour flight to Montreal aboard a propeller-driven plane, I was fortunate to be seated next to a friendly Canadian couple returning home from a European vacation. They were curious about my story and thought it romantic and exciting.

Where did this desire to see the world come from, this discontent with the narrowness of life in the six counties of Ulster? I was young. I craved adventure and excitement. I wanted to escape Northern Ireland's narrow boundaries, its legacy of hatred and intolerance, perpetuated in smug remarks cloaked in blankets of bigotry. How easy it is to put people into watertight compartments as if they were boarding a train where each has his own preordained destination.

I wanted to go where nobody knew me, for I came from a country so small that the first round of social inter-course consisted of poking and prying into your background until your religion, your education, and your social status were established. But the history of the Irish is also the story of emigration. Most Irish families have relatives who have sought their fortunes around the world, especially in the countries that formed part of the British Empire.

My father's brother Harold had gone to Australia at twenty years of age and had never returned. Granny Morrow wrote to all her brothers and sisters who had scattered to Canada, Australia and New Zealand. She read me their letters and those from Uncle Harold. She explained who everyone was in the photograph albums. I was most impressed with the first pictures of Uncle Harold in Australia, bare-chested, felling gigantic trees in the steaming tropical heat of Queensland, so different from Northern Ireland.

At school my favorite subject was geography. I loved to draw maps, I yearned to visit India with its sacred river the Ganges or travel to South America and explore its mighty Amazon. It fired my imagination to learn about other countries. I pored over stories of adventure from Robert Louis Stevenson's *Robinson Crusoe* to accounts of discovery, of expeditions to the

North Pole, to exotic lands, of the conquest of Mount Everest. The tedium of my daily life was forgotten as I accompanied Thor Heyerdahl and his raft on the Kon-Tiki Expedition to the South Seas. One of my favorite books, a Sunday school prize, was a thin book with a pale blue cover called *Lives That Moved the World*. I was inspired by the bravery and daring of Edith Cavell, Florence Nightingale and the great explorers of Africa, Rhodes and Stanley. I trembled for the safety of the members of the French resistance and the escaped German prisoners of war, in the tales of World War II.

I was growing up after "The War," as it was called, when the British Empire was more or less intact. Society was changing in the U.K. and Northern Ireland, and the Labour Party was in power in England. Fortunately, I was born in 1936, and so had the opportunity to attend high school and later Queen's University in Belfast. For working class families life had suddenly changed for the better. Older people were able to collect pensions; the health service was introduced; people no longer worried about being put in the poorhouse or not being able to afford a doctor. Many people went to the dentist for the first time in their lives, other than to get all their teeth pulled out. Higher education was no longer restricted to those who could pay for it, or the fortunate few who were granted scholarships.

It was at Queen's that I decided I wasn't staying in N. Ireland. With an Arts Degree, there were not many alternatives to teaching, especially for women. I contemplated going to England, but didn't really relish the idea of imprisoning myself in a girls' boarding school. I was, after all, trying to escape the confines of a narrow world. I remained at the university for the Diploma in Education. One of the conditions for this scholarship was a promise to teach for two years in Northern Ireland; so the decision to leave was postponed for a short time. However, the desire increased, inflamed by job offerings posted on the Education Department's notice board for exotic places like St. Kitts and Barbados. It grew to mammoth proportions while I taught at the Girls' Model Secondary Modern School in Belfast.

During my second year there, I began to plan my escape. Each Thursday *The London Times* published the *Educational Supplement* where jobs around the world were advertised. In a fever of excitement I would comb the ads, trying to decide if I should go to the Caribbean, the Canadian Rockies, possibly Turkey, maybe Australia or New Zealand. The possibilities seemed endless.

There were, unfortunately, a few practical considerations. I had no money other than my salary, which at the time was not very large. Women were paid less than men and each month I sent money home to my mother to help support the family. My father had died just a few years earlier. Bertha and I were the only two children working.

As the oldest child, the ever responsible support for my mother, I had wrestled with my conscience as to whether I could or should go. Finally I decided that I owed it to myself to try. I would return in two or three years. In the meantime

Harold, who was a year and a half younger than I and who was graduating as an engineer that same year, could shoulder some of the responsibility that I had always assumed.

In those days teachers were scarce in many countries, and many would offer to pay the cost of the fare in return for a contract of two or three years. This was the route I had to take. My choice began to narrow. Australia was too far away, no one ever returned from there. I had a very good Malayan friend with whom I had shared an apartment and who hoped to return to Malaya as soon as she finished her studies. I applied for a teaching job with the British Army in Malaya.

However, I had to have a reference from my headmistress. If I went to Miss Craig, she would know I was thinking of leaving. Rules and etiquette regarding jobs were strict; this was a strict school and she was a strict headmistress. Schools expected at least three months notice of resignation in order to have the pick of new graduates for their roster of teachers before school closed for the summer.

I flew to London for the interview at the War Office. It was my first time in an airplane, my first real adventure alone. (The previous summer I had gone to Spain with some teachers, but traveled by boat, train and bus. The journey had taken three days.) The interview was at a long oak table surrounded by army officers in a huge paneled conference room complete with portraits of imposing-looking generals on the walls.

The interview went well until the only female officer present emphasized the fact that I was the oldest daughter of a widow with young children. She insisted that my mother would send for me if a problem arose. I knew that this was probably not true, but could not find the words to convince this formidable woman. I was not surprised when I received their letter of regret.

Now I had a serious problem. Miss Craig wanted to know if I was going to the army. Having decided on something more exotic, I had missed interviews for teaching in Canada and Australia. Representatives from these countries used to come to N. Ireland and England each spring in their search for teachers. I decided to take the plunge.

I handed in my resignation, to the horror of the head-mistress and my flat-mate Connie. Finding jobs was at a pre-mium, the atmosphere was ultra-conservative, and worst of all I was one of the two children in the family who was now work-ing. I was the daughter for whose university education my mother had sacrificed. But I couldn't bear to return to that narrow-minded school, or to spend the rest of my life in wet, dreary N. Ireland and probably end up as the old maid aunt in this large family of brothers and sisters. I didn't dare tell my family what I had done, least of all my mother.

In January of that year 1960, I had bumped into Ian Mahood at a dance at Queen's. He was a friend Harold's; they had shared digs together, and that year were living at Queen's Elms, the men's residence. Ian informed me that he was plan-ning to work abroad after graduation, and as I was also in my planning period, we had a lot in common.

I wasn't interested in a romantic relationship, but I had always liked Ian and when he invited me to a dance or the movies, I thought "Why not?" I was warned by Harold that Ian was a really decent fellow, and ... What he meant by that, I never was quite sure, because I didn't see myself as the "femme fatale dancing the tango in stiletto heels with a red rose between my teeth, breaking the hearts of my victims."

Well, one thing led to another, and in May he asked if I would wait for him for two years as he had a job offer in Saudi Arabia. This was after my momentous decision to resign, about which he knew nothing. At first I said I would, but the prospect was not exciting; a lot could happen in two years. Then he was given two other possibilities to consider: studying for a Master's degree in Scotland or working in Montreal. We finally decided on Montreal. Scotland was too much like home, and Saudi Arabia was not for women.

On a blue airmail letter, I wrote to the Protestant School Board of Greater Montreal telling them about myself and inquiring about possible job opportunities. Within a few weeks I received an offer of employment as a Math and English teacher, starting in September. I was overjoyed. For those who couldn't afford the airfare, the school board had an arrangement to deduct it in installments from the first year's salary. Things were working out; now I had to find somewhere cheap to stay for a few days. Ian's employer, Northern Electric, had paid his fare and arranged for him to stay at the YMCA until he got settled. Engineers were always better remunerated than teachers. I wrote to the YWCA and booked a room for a week.

He left for Canada two weeks before me. I couldn't afford to spend a few weeks in Montreal before starting work. I arrived on Monday, the fourth of September and had to report to the Town of Mount Royal High School the next morning for my assignment and teacher orientation. I started teaching the following day.

Ian had assured me that he would be at the airport to meet me. In Montreal, the couple I had met on the plane helped me with luggage and customs and to find Ian. No Ian! I had never considered this possibility; I had perfect faith in his trustworthiness. My new friends tried to calm me, to point out that it was only five o'clock in the morning and that probably the first limos were not running yet. This was indeed the case.

After checking into the YWCA, Ian and I spent the day together. We went to my new school on the subway, so that I would know where to go in the morning; we walked around Montreal, and sat in parks. I couldn't bear to be left alone, and he couldn't enter the YWCA.

We never did return to live in N. Ireland, and the desire to see the world never diminished. Ian and I have had an interesting life together, and the six month relationship with no strings attached has become a lasting marriage. Because of his job, we have had the opportunity to live in four other countries and learn two new languages. We have furniture that has traveled more miles than most people.

Youth does not think of all the consequences of its actions, and perhaps it is just as well. I have missed family and friends over the years. I don't have the same sense of identity as someone, who has lived in one country all his or her life. To the Irish, I'm a Yank; to the Americans, I'm Irish. To myself, I'm a rolling stone that has gathered some moss.

> But I have promises to keep,
> And miles to go before I sleep.
> And miles to go before I sleep.
> —Robert Frost

Deer Isle

Maine, USA

Ireland taught me restraint.

On the coast of Maine, my horizons
are reversed, flipped
like a coin with two faces.
The Atlantic still churns
in its diurnal consistency,
pulverizing what lies in its path.

Like wrack I had drifted
from a present layered
in the bitter sediment of history.

But here, on this edge of the North
Atlantic, I find pinions and stanchions
in granite and trees where the sea
offers constant renewal
to cream and gray rocks on the shore.

The ocean moans in its troughs
laps a rhythmic cadence,
lacy foam curling round tide-washed stones.
And wind stirs scented pines
that hunker down to the water
keening and singing.

Epilogue

Only two of Mother's children, Bertha and Marcella, stayed in N. Ireland. Four of her sons; Harold, Derek, Clifford and Trevor, migrated to Great Britain. Noel lives in Jakarta, Indonesia, and the author of these memoirs, Beatrice, now resides in N. Carolina, U.S.A. Mother would be proud to know that her descendants, children and grandchildren, are well represented in the professional and business worlds.

The house at 24 Milburn Street no longer exists. A few years after Mother's death it and the adjoining house fell into disrepair and finally were demolished. The long, narrow gardens have become a luxury housing estate, called Millane Manor.

Glossary

Blether	talk nonsense; brag; tell tales
Ceilidh house;	a friendly visit to a neighbor's go visiting; chat or gossip
Craic, crack	talk; gossip
Hard wrought	hard worked
Kep the cows (animals)	stop, turn aside, head off
Och	*an exclamation* expressing sorrow, regret, weariness, impatience etc. *verb* to utter this exclamation e.g. What are ye ochin about?
Sheugh	a drainage channel in a field or alongside a road; a small stream
Sup o' tay	a cup of tea

Thanks

Many people encouraged and helped me with this book. I would like to thank my teacher at N.C. State University, Dr. David Covington, who first pointed me in the right direction and suggested I collect my memoirs in a book. My special thanks go to my teachers and friends at Meredith College: Betty Adcock, Dr. Ione Knight and Lou Rosser for their suggestions and editing. Also to Way Poteat for his computer skills and Jillian Miller for restoration of the old photographs. Lastly to my husband Ian and brother Clifford, who have been such enthusiastic supporters over the years.

Acknowledgments to the *Raleigh News and Observer* for publishing the article *Where I come from* and to the literary magazine *Natural Bridge* for publishing the poem *Deer Isle*.

Contributor

B etty Adcock, who wrote the Prologue, is an American poet and a 2002–2003 Guggenheim Fellow. Author of six poetry collections, she has served as a faculty member in the Warren Wilson Program for Writers in Asheville, NC and in the Writer-in-Residence program at Meredith College in Raleigh, NC.

Made in the USA
Charleston, SC
15 November 2010